1908

Mother
From Lizzie
Xmas 1912

Harold Frank Knowles
Purchased at Oakland,
10-31-1959

#24⁰⁰/R
#005

ISLE OF WIGHT

A. HEATON COOPER

THE NEEDLES

ISLE OF WIGHT

PAINTED BY

A. HEATON COOPER

DESCRIBED BY

A. R. HOPE MONCRIEFF

LONDON

ADAM AND CHARLES BLACK

1908

Contents

List of Illustrations

vii

Isle of Wight

Map at end of volume

ISLE OF WIGHT

THE ISLAND

The Island, as its people are in the way of styling it, while not going so far as to deny existence to the adjacent islands of Great Britain and Ireland—the Wight, as it is sometimes called by old writers—has for the first fact in its history that it was not always an island. It once made a promontory of Dorset, cut off from the mainland by a channel, whose rush of encountering tides seems still wearing away the shores so as to broaden a passage of half a dozen miles at the most, narrowed to about a mile between the long spit of Hurst and the north-western corner of the Island. It may be that what is now a strait has been the estuary of a great river, flooding itself into the sea, which, like Hengist and Horsa, is apt to prove an invading ally difficult to get rid of. *Wight* is taken to represent an old British name for the channel, that, by monkish Latinists, came to be christened *pelagus solvens;* but the Solent may have had rather some etymological kinship with the Solway.

The Channel Island, as thus its full style imports,

1   A

Isle of Wight

has a natural history of singular interest to geologists, who find here a wide range of fossiliferous strata, from the Upper Eocene to the Wealden clay, so exposed that one scientific authority admiringly declares how it "might have been cut out by nature for a geological model illustrative of the principles of stratification." Perhaps the general reader may thank a writer for not enlarging on this head; but a few words must be said about the geological structure that shapes this Island's scenery, forming, as it were, a sort of abridged and compressed edition of no small part of England. It divides itself into three zones, which may be traced in the same order upon the Isle of Purbeck in Dorset. Through the centre runs a backbone of chalk Downs, a few hundred feet high and an hour's walk across at the broadest, narrowing towards either end to crumble into the sea at the white cliffs of Culver and of the Needles. To the south of this come beds of sand and marl, through which the chalk again bulges out in isolated masses on the south coast to top the highest crests of the Island, resting on such an unstable foundation that extensive landslips here have thrown the architecture of nature into picturesque ruin. The north side in general is tamer, a plain of clays dotted by gravel, better wooded than the rest, though much of its old timber has gone into the wooden walls of England, once kept in repair at Portsmouth.

Across these zones of length, the Island is cut into

The Island

two almost equal parts by its chief river, the Medina, cleaving the central Downs near Newport; and through gaps at either end flow two smaller rivers bearing the same name of Yar, which seems to call Celtic cousinship with the Garonne of France. For the Medina, as for the Medway, some such derivation as the *Mid* stream has been naturally suggested; but with the fear of Dr Bradley upon me, I would pass lightly over the quaking bog of place nomenclature. These three rivers have the peculiarity of flowing almost right across the Island, a course so short that they may well take their time about it. The other streams are of little importance, except in the way of scenery. On the north side they form shallow branching creeks which get from as much as they give to the sea, that at high tide bears brown sails far inland among trees and hedges. On the south, wearing their way down through the elevated shore line, they carve out those abrupt chasms known as Chines, celebrated among the beauty spots of this coast. The richest valley seems to be that of the larger Yar, which turns into the sea at the north-east corner. The parts most rich in natural charms are the south-eastern corner, with its overgrown landslips, and the fissured chalk cliffs of the western promontory beyond Freshwater.

All that variety of soil and surface is packed together into a roughly rhomboidal shape, 23 miles long by 13 or 14 miles at the broadest, about the size of Greater London, or say $\frac{1}{36000}$ part of the

Isle of Wight

habitable globe. Within its circumference of 60 miles
or so, this space of some 96,000 square acres holds
a population of 82,000, beside innumerable transient
visitors. A pundit of figures has taken the trouble
to calculate that all the population of the world could
find standing room in the Island on the foot of four
to the square yard, if the human race agreed on
spending a Bank Holiday here; but then little room
might be left for donkey-rides or switch-back railways. While we are on the head of statistics, it
may be mentioned that several scores of guide-books
to the Isle of Wight have been published, from Sir
Henry Englefield's noble folio to the small brochures
issued by hotels, these works containing on an
average 206,732 words, mostly superfluous in many
cases; that 810,427 picture post-cards or thereabouts
pass annually through the post-offices of the island;
that, in ordinary seasons, it sits to 1723 cameras;
that the hotel-bills annually paid in it would, if
tacked together, reach from St Petersburg to Yoko-
hama, or if pasted over one another, make a pile
as high as the new War Office; and that 11·059
per cent. of the newly married couples of Brixton,
Balham, Upper Tooting, etc., are in each year
estimated to spend at least part of their honeymoon
here, who come back to confirm a prevailing belief
that in no other part of the British Isles does the
moon shine so sweetly; while, indeed, a not quite
clearly ascertained proportion of them live to assert
that the scenery of the Island and the happiness of

the marriage state have alike been more or less over-rated. I give these figures for what they are worth, along with the unquestioned fact that the Isle of Wight belongs, in a manner, to the county of Hants, but has a County Council of its own, and in general maintains a very insular attitude of independence, modelled on the proud bearing of Great Britain towards mere continental countries.

Facts and figures somewhat fail one who comes to lecture on the original population of this Island. The opinion fondly held in a certain section of "smart" society, that the lawn of the Squadron at Cowes represents the Garden of Eden, seems to rest upon no critical authority; indeed Adam and Eve, as owners of no yacht, would not be qualified for admission to this select enclosure. With some confidence we may state that the Island was first peopled by aborigines enjoying no protection against kidnappers and conquerors, who themselves found it difficult in the long run to blackball undesirable aliens, as Australia and New Zealand try to do under the protection of fleets steaming forth from the Solent. There are well-marked indications of invasion by a Belgic tribe from the mainland, to make this a "free" state, as early prelude to King Leopold's civilisation of the Congo. But we may pass lightly over the Celtic period, with place-names and pit-dwellings as its records, to come into clearer historic light with Vespasian's conquest in A.D. 43.

For more than three centuries, with apparently

one episode of revolt, the Romans held Vectis, as they called it; and it has been maintained, though this goes not unquestioned, that here was their *Ictis* port, at which they shipped the tin drawn from the mines of Cornwall. If so, the island described by Diodorus Siculus was then an island only at high water. The clearest marks left by Rome are the remains of villas unearthed at different points, at least one of which indicates a tenant of luxurious habits and tastes. We can understand how Italian exiles might prefer this station to one in the bleak wilds of Derbyshire or Northumberland, as an Anglo-Indian official of to-day thinks himself lucky to have his compound at Poona or Bangalore, if not at Mahableshwar or Simla. The Brading villa, indeed, like those of Bignor in Sussex and Brough in Norfolk, seems rather to have been the settled home of a rich nobleman, Roman or Romanised British, who had perhaps strong opinions as to the way in which Rome neglected the wishes and interests of her colonies. These remains were unearthed only in living memory, so that writers of a century ago ignore such traces of Roman occupation.

Next came northern pirates, who would be not so much interested in the mild climate of the Island, as in the creeks and landing-places of its shores. They, too, have left relics of their occupation, chiefly in the graves furnished with utensils and ornaments of heathen life. But when Jutes and Saxons had destroyed the Roman civilisation, they fell under

another influence spread from the Mediterranean.
Bishop Wilfred of Selsey has the credit of planting,
or replanting, Christianity in the Island. It could
hardly have taken deep root, when the Danes came
to ravage the monastic settlements. For a time the
Cross and the Raven must have struggled for
mastery here like the encountering tides of Solent,
till that new wave of invaders ebbed back or was
absorbed into the old one; then again the Island
became overflowed by a fresh storm of conquest.
If we consider from how many races, in three continents, the Roman soldiery were drawn, and how the
northmen must have mixed their blood with that of
a miscellany of captives, it is clear that, when overrun by a fresh cross-breed between Gauls and
Vikings, the population of our islands, large and
small, could in many parts have been no very pure
stock, such as is fondly imagined by the pride of
modern Pan-Celticism and Anglo-Saxondom.

In Norman England, the Wight soon emerges
into note. King William visited it to seize his
ambitious brother Odo at Carisbrooke. The fortress there was enlarged by William Fitz-Osborne,
to whom the Island had been granted, and who
salved his conscience for any high-handed acts of
conquest by giving six churches to the Norman
Abbey of Lira, the beginning of a close connection
with that continental foundation. His son lost this
lordship through treason; then for two centuries it
was in the hands of the Redvers, Earls of Devon,

who grew to be quasi-independent princes. The last of their line was Isabella de Fortibus, holding her head high as Lady of the Island till on her deathbed, her children being dead, she sold her rights to Edward I. for 6000 marks.

Henceforth this dependency was governed for the crown through lieutenants at first known as Wardens, an office held by great names like Edward III. in his childhood, the Earl of Salisbury, the Duke of York, the Duke of Gloucester, Anthony Woodvile, Earl of Rivers; and in such hands more than once showing a tendency to become hereditary. Their post was no sinecure, for at this period the Island made a striking point for French raids that have left their mark on its towns. Not that the raiding was all on one side. The islanders long remembered ruefully how Sir Edward Woodvile led the flower of their manhood into France, when of more than four hundred fighters only one boy escaped to tell the tale of their destruction, that seems to have been wrought by French artillery, turning the tables on the English long-bow.

The weak Henry VI. had crowned young Henry Beauchamp, Duke of Warwick, as "King of the Isle of Wight." Politic Henry VII., for his part, saw well to restrain the power and dignity of those Island deputies, now styled Captains. In the Tudor time, three Captains came to note, Sir Richard Worsley as carrying out the reformation policy of Henry VIII., Sir Edward Horsey, as a doughty soldier of fortune, who is said to have begun his career with a plot to betray the Island to the French, but on coming into this office kept a sharp eye both on foreign enemies and on his private interests, doing a bit of piracy for his own hand, if all stories be true; then Sir George Carey, who had the anxious task of defence against the Spanish Armada. When that peril went to pieces, the Island at last began to enjoy a period of secure prosperity, testified to by the fact that most of its old houses, mansion or cottage, appear to date from Elizabeth or James. Yet so late as 1627, soon after the captaincy of Lord Southampton, Shakespeare's patron, it got a scare from a Dutch fleet, taken for Spaniards.

New confusion came with the Civil War, in which the Wight people were mostly on the parliament's side, while the leading gentry stood for the king. The best-known episode of the Island's history is Charles I.'s imprisonment at Carisbrooke, which may be passed over here to be dealt with more fully *in loco*. The Isle of Wight might well back up the parliament; as then and till the Reform Bill it sent six members, an over-representation now reduced to one, and formerly, indeed, apt to be qualified by official interference with freedom of election.

In Charles II.'s "golden age of the coward, the bigot and the slave," the governorship of the Island was given to Lord Colepeper, who made himself obnoxious here, and got a wider field of domination in Virginia, where also he seems to have been unbeloved. His huge colonial grants passed by marriage of his daughter to Lord Fairfax, whose eldest son settled on his American property, said to extend over five million acres, giving up the English estates to his younger brother. This was clearly hint for Thackeray's story of the Virginian Warringtons. Only the other day the heir of this family, America's sole peer, became naturalised afresh in England, after his title had been laid up in lavender, or tobacco, for several generations. Another personage in *The Virginians*, General Webb, held the governorship of the Island for a few years. But now the Captains, or Governors as they came to be styled, had little to do which could not be done by deputy, while the post was worth holding by men of high rank, as by the Dukes of Bolton and Montague under George II., when its salary was £1500 a year.

Under them the Island was happy enough to have little history, though it had again to be on its guard when Dutch admirals talked of sweeping the English ships from the Channel. It saw William's fleet sail by on the way to Torbay; and two years later it seemed about to have from its southern cliffs the spectacle of a hundred French sail engaging the English and Dutch squadrons; but the scene of that encounter was shifted to Beachy Head, where it ended in a manner not much dwelt upon in our naval annals. Then the long struggle with Napoleon once more turned this outpost of England into a camp. In the peaceful days that followed, the governorship became a mere ceremonial function. The title, held by Prince Henry of Battenberg, was passed on to his widow, the youngest daughter of Queen Victoria, whose death at Osborne makes the last date in this Island chronicle.

An insulated people naturally formed a race apart, speaking a marked dialect, and cherishing a strong local feeling. Their situation, and the once pressing need to stand on defence by land and sea, bred a sturdy race, whose vigour in old days was apt to run to such enterprising ways of life as piracy, wrecking, and smuggling; but all that may be forgotten like scandal about Queen Elizabeth. One evil of the islanders keeping so much to themselves has been a stagnation of population, that through intermarriage made for degeneracy. Sir John Oglander, the Stuart worthy whose jottings on his contemporaries prove so amusing, says that the Island once bore the reproach of not producing a good horse, a wise man, or a pretty woman; but he hastens to add *Tempora mutant;* and on the last head, the stranger can judge the calumny for himself. Hassell, an eighteenth century tourist, remarks for his part on the beauty and even elegance of the farmers' daughters at Newport market, while of the fathers he hints at grog-blossoms as a too common feature. The lately published memoirs of Captain Elers treat the former point as matter of notoriety. A certain boisterous pertness noted in the male

11

youth of the Island has been referred by sociologists
to an absence of birch in its flora. All ages have
been noted for a clannishness that was once disposed
to look askance on such "overners" or "overers"
as found their way into the Wight, whose own stock
we see to have sprung from immigrants of different
breeds. But here, as elsewhere, schools, newspapers,
and facilities of travel are fast rubbing down the
prejudices of parish patriotism.

The upper class, indeed, is now largely made up
of well-to-do strangers drawn to the Island by its
various amenities; while the sons of the soil have
laid aside suspicious dislike of the outsiders whom
they know as profitable guests. From pictorial
cards, valentines, and such vulgar documents, they
appear to bear the nickname of Isle of Wight
"Calves," which may be taken as a sub-species of
the "Hampshire Hogs," who suffer such neighbourly satire as is shown in by-words like "Norfolk
Dumplings," "Lincolnshire Yellow-bellies," or
"Wiltshire Moonrakers." Some strangers, however, at the height of the season, have been more
inclined to find for the natives a zoological similitude
in the order of *Raptores*. "I do not mean," as a
precise old gentleman once explained to me of his
landlady, "that she has feathers and claws like a
bird; but I assert that, in character and in disposition, she resembles a vulture." It is often, indeed,
made evident to the meanest capacity that the
Island hosts belong to a long-billed family; but they

The Island

perhaps as often as not may be classed as overners, or referred to the hydra-like form of polyzoic organism popularly known as a Company, Limited.

The soil is well cultivated, and many of the farms look thriving, though the rank hedges and the flowers that colour some of the pastures, spread a more pleasing view for an idle stranger than for a practical cultivator. The Downs support flocks as well as golf clubs; the breed of Island sheep was highly esteemed of old, where the climate makes for early lambing. When some parts were overrun with "conies," Sir E. Horsey had the name of bringing in hares, which he paid for at the rate of a lamb a-piece; but foxes and badgers have not crossed the Solent.

The coast folk carry on amphibious business, from oyster beds to ship-chandling. Ship-building at Cowes, and cement-making on the Medina, are the only large industries I know of. The chief trade seems to be in tourists, who are taxed, tolled, and touted for at every turn by the purveyors of entertainment for man and beast, the managers of excursions, and the enclosers of natural curiosities. Visitors come from far and near, the Island making a holiday resort for the townsfolk of Portsmouth and Southampton, while among foreign tourists, it seems to have a special attraction for Germans; and some of the American travellers who "do" Europe in three weeks are known to spend as much as several hours in scampering across to Ventnor.

Isle of Wight

A good many visitors, however, come for a considerable time, delicate or luxurious folk, lucky enough to be able to take advantage of a milder climate in our uncertain winter or still more treacherous spring. One must not indeed expect too much of any British climate. About Torquay, the chief rival of Ventnor as a sheltered resort, a well-known novelist, after living there through many winters, says bluntly that it is a little less cold than the rest of England. Such places are apt to bid for patronage by statistics of sunshine, temperature, and so forth, which may prove bamboozling, not to say deceptive, when it is difficult to tabulate the occurrence of trying extremes under the changes and chances of our fickle sky. The best test of climate is its general effect on vegetation; and it may be said with truth that the Isle of Wight, on the whole, is two or three weeks ahead of inland districts of our country. But it cannot claim to be such a halcyon spot as the dream-world of another poet, who knew it well in all weathers.

> The island-valley of Avilion,
> Where falls not hail, or rain, or any snow,
> Nor any wind blows loudly, but it lies
> Deep-meadowed, happy, fair with orchard lawns
> And bowery hollows crowned with summer sea.

There is snow here, sometimes, and rain pretty often; while wind makes for the islanders as touchy a point as the title "Lady of Snows" for Canada; but in fact, being an island, this nook must take the

The Island

consequences of such a situation, swept by breezes from all quarters, especially from the south-west. The north and east sides of course are more exposed to bracing winds, and their resorts, from Cowes to Sandown, come into favour rather in the summer season, that fills the sails of yachts and pleasure-boats, as well as greases the wheels of coaches cruising upon land excursions. The "Back of the Island" is more stormed upon by Atlantic gales, while one half of it, the famous Undercliff, is so snugly shut in to the north, as to make a winter garden of myrtles, fuchsias, arbutus, and still rarer evergreenery. Here, perhaps, it was that a Miss Malaprop complained of this Island as not "embracing" enough, and got advice to try then the Isle of Man.

As to the best time for a visit, that depends partly on which aspect of the Island is to be sought, not to say on circumstances and opportunity; but to my mind it wears its fairest face in its dullest season, when its hotel-keepers see cause to take their own holiday. Then, in early summer, flocks of sheep-like tourists miss seeing at their freshest and richest the clumps of umbrageous foliage, the hedgerows and copses sweet with gay blossoms, the turfy slopes spangled with wild flowers, the glowing meadows, the blooming cottage plots, the "weeds of glorious feature," and in short, all the charms that make this one of "the gardens of England," in which, exclaims Oliver Wendell Holmes, "everything grows with such a lavish extravagance of greenery that it seems

15

as if it must bankrupt the soil before autumn." It is better visited in spring, which comes so early up this way, that Easter as well as Whitsuntide holiday-makers may catch the first flush of one of those nooks described by Dr Bromfield in his *Flora Vectensis*— "a blooming wilderness of primroses, wood-anemones, violets, and a hundred other lovely and fragrant things, overtopped by the taller and purple-stained wood-spurge, early purple orchis, and the pointed hoods of the spotted-leaved wake-robin; the daisy-besprinkled track leading us upward, skirted by mossy fern-clad banks on one hand, and by shelving thickets on the other, profusely overshadowed by ivy-arched oak and ash, the graceful birch, and varnished holly." Then still sooner may be looked for the spangling of the sheltered Undercliff, where, as Miss Sewell describes : " The ground is tossed about in every direction, and huge rocks lie scattered upon it. But thorns and chestnuts and ash-trees have sprung up amongst them upon the greensward ; ivy has climbed up the ledges of the jagged cliffs ; primroses cluster upon the banks ; cowslips glitter on the turf; and masses of hyacinths may be seen in glades, half hidden by the foliage of the thick trees, through which the jutting masses of grey rock peep out upon the open sea, sparkling with silver and blue some hundreds of feet beneath them."

Old books frequently dwell on what was once a drawback, the difficulty of getting to the Island—the getting away from which is more apparent to one class of his present Majesty's subjects, housed here at Parkhurst, much against their will. Piers and steamboats have now made it as accessible as the Isle of Thanet, and more often visited than the Isle of Dogs. There are half-a-dozen routes from London, through the three opposite ports of Portsmouth, Southampton, and Lymington, not to speak of Southsea and Stokes Bay. The Portsmouth route comes into closest touch with the Island's own railways, made up of several local enterprises, amalgamated into the two systems styled the Isle of Wight Railway, and the Isle of Wight Central Railway. Of these lines the Rev. Mr Chadband would be bound to say that they are perhaps the worst, the dearest, and the most provoking in the country; to which their shareholders could reply only by a groan worthy of Mr Stiggins, while a want of mutual connection and convenience may be referred to relations like those of Messrs Jorkins and Spenlow. From their exactions it is the hasty stranger that suffers most, the inhabitants being better versed in devices of season-tickets, parliamentary fares, and other mitigations of a tariff, by which, for example, it costs sixpence to go from one end of Ryde Pier to the other, and half-a-crown or so for the dozen miles' trip across the Island.

But if the visitor grudge such charges, he will find plenty of competition in the excursion coaches that gape for him as soon as he gets off Ryde Pier, or the motor 'buses that hence ply in several directions.

Isle of Wight

For his own wheel there are excellent roads, as well
as others; and to see the best of the Island, he does
well if he can avail himself of that oldest and cheapest
conveyance known to merry hearts as "Shanks'
mare." It is on this footing, chiefly, that I have
wandered about the Isle of Wight, through which I
am now to conduct the gentle reader on a rambling
and gossiping tour in his own arm-chair.

RYDE

We need not cast about for the spot at which to make our landing on the shores of Wight. Lying opposite Portsmouth, with a crossing of half-an-hour or so, Ryde is the chief gateway of the Island and knot of its railways to every part, Cowes being more in touch with Southampton, and Yarmouth at the west end coming closest to the mainland port of Lymington. With its suburbs and dependencies, Ryde is considerably the largest place, having outgrown Newport, the titular capital, by a population largely made up of retired veterans, families of officers on service, and other select society such as one finds thickly settled at Southsea, across the Solent. So much one can guess from the look of the brick villas that spread over the swelling heights of Ryde's background, and of the smart shops in and about its Union Street, while an unusual proportion of hotels and refreshment rooms hint at influx of transient visitors both from the classes and the masses.

A century ago, this could be described in a local guide-book as a "place of some consequence." Only since then has Ryde become the goodly town we now see, yet it is no mushroom resort, but old enough to have been burned by French assailants under Richard II. The sheltered anchorage behind the Isle of Wight was once too well known to wind-bound travellers, who might have to fret here for weeks or months, as Leigh Hunt, on his voyage to Italy, spent half a year at Plymouth. So Fielding, sailing to die at Lisbon, was detained at Ryde, which seems then to have been little more than a hamlet. No tea could be got there; it had a butcher, but he was not "killing"; and though the inn at which the travellers put up could supply a long bill, its other accommodations were such that they preferred to take their dinner in the barn. The landing of a helpless invalid proved a trying adventure where, "between the sea and the shore, there was at low water an impassable gulf, if I may so call it, of deep mud, which could neither be traversed by walking nor swimming, so that for near one half of the twenty-four hours, Ryde was inaccessible by friend or foe." In spite of such disadvantages, the dying novelist has nothing but good to say of it, once he had got over its moat of mud.

This pleasant village is situated on a gentle ascent from the water, whence it affords that charming prospect I have above described. Its soil is a gravel, which, assisted with its declivity, preserves it always so dry, that immediately after the most violent rain, a fine lady may walk without wetting her silken shoes. The fertility of the place is apparent from its extraordinary verdure, and it is so shaded with large and flourishing elms, that its narrow lanes are a

RYDE—MOONRISE

Ryde

natural grove or walk, which in the regularity of its plantation vies
with the power of art, and in its wanton exuberancy greatly exceeds
it. In a field, in the ascent of this hill, about a quarter of a mile from
the sea, stands a neat little chapel. It is very small, but adequate to
the number of inhabitants : for the parish doth not seem to contain
above thirty houses.

Marryat also speaks of the muddy shore, over
which voyagers had often to be carried ashore pick-
aback or in a horse and cart, as was the way of landing at Buenos Ayres till not so long ago. But he
saw the construction of its pier, one of the earliest
pleasure piers in England, that made a great difference to Ryde; and for a time it shot up into more
note and fashion as a seaside resort than it enjoys
now among so many rivals. A hint of that palmy
time is given by some dignified old mansions about
the town, which, during the last half century or so,
has looked for quantity as much as quality in its
visitors.

At the present day, the bed of mud has been
overlaid by a coat of sand, taken advantage of for
bathing facilities still too dependent on the tide,
ebbing out beyond an unfinished pier that serves as a
swimming bath at certain hours. By means of
groynes, the sand is now being coaxed to gather less
thinly on the shore, where a battery of bathing
machines stands in position. Else Ryde is no very
good bathing place ; nor, exposed to cold winds, does
it invite invalids like the other side of the Island. Its
interests have been rather in yachting and boating ;
and its frequenters those who relish a breezy marine

flavour in life. August, gay with regattas, is the great time for this Solent shore. The broad pier, 2000 feet long, sets the tide at defiance, carrying out both a railway and a tramway to meet the steamers that land holiday crowds as well as passengers for all parts of the Island. For the amusement of youthful visitors a canoeing lake has been made in the gardens, behind the sea-wall running eastwards, with its fine view of Spithead and the chequered forts islanded in the Solent.

It was off this Esplanade that in 1782 went down the *Royal George*, one of our finest men-of-war, upset by a land breeze when heeled over safely enough, as was supposed, in calm weather. The story goes that a pig-headed officer of the watch would not attend to the carpenter's report that she was filling; then naval discipline cost the loss of seven hundred lives. Great numbers of bodies came ashore at Ryde, to be buried under what is now a trim promenade. Others found a resting-place in Portsea Churchyard, where a monument to their memory stands under the noble tower of the new Church, so well seen from the railway as it enters Portsmouth. The catastrophe is best remembered by Cowper's epitaph, "Toll for the Brave!" and by the narrative in Marryat's *Poor Jack*. Less well known are Sir Henry Englefield's lines, written when the graves could still be seen near the shore.

> Thou! who dost tread this smooth and verdant mead,
> Viewing delighted the fair hills that rise

Ryde

On either hand, a sylvan theatre ;
While in the front with snowy pinions closed,
And thunders silent, Britain's guardian fleet
On the deep bosom of the azure sea
Reposes aweful—pass not heedless by
These mould'ring heaps, which the blue spiry grass
Scarce guards from mingling with the common earth.
Mark ! in how many a melancholy rank.
The graves are marshall'd—Dost thou know the fate
Disastrous, of their tenants ?   Hushed the winds,
And smooth the billows, when an unseen hand
Smote the great ship, and rift her massy beams :
She reeled and sunk.—Over her swarming decks
The flashing wave in horrid whirlpool rushed ;
While from a thousand throats, one wailing shriek
Burst—and was heard no more.
     Then day by day,
The ebbing tide left frequent on the sand,
The livid corpse ; and his o'erloaded net
The shuddering fisher loathed to drag ashore.
And here, by friends unknown, unmarked, unwept,
They rest." [1]

Another event in Ryde's history was the landing
here of the Empress of the French after Sedan.   Her
escape from Paris had been conducted by Dr Evans,
the American dentist ; then from Deauville, Sir John

[1] The poet adds a footnote of facts. "The ship, when first she
filled, fell over so as to dip the flag at her masthead into the sea.
Then rolling back, she fell over to the other side till her yard-arms
touched the water.   She then righted, and sunk nearly upright.
While she was sinking, nearly every soul on board came on deck ;
and I was told by Admiral Sotheby, then a lieutenant on board the
next ship, that as she went down, this mass of people gave a cry so
lamentable, that it was still ringing in his ears. It was supposed
that at the time of the accident, above a thousand persons, men and
women, were on board ; not four hundred were saved.   The eddy
made by the sinking ship was so great that a large victualling barge
which lay alongside was drawn in, and lost with her."

23

Isle of Wight

Burgoyne brought her across in his yacht through such stormy weather, that it had almost been forced to put back into some French port. At sunrise, a Ryde hotel close to the pier turned away two travel-worn ladies accompanied by a gentleman, who found refuge in the York Hotel. So the unfortunate Empress, with her small suite, could at last rest in peace. The first thing she did, Dr Evans tells us, was to seek comfort in a Bible that, by chance as she supposed, lay in the small top room given to this *incognita*. Charles X. on his final exile, had also made for the Isle of Wight, arriving off Cowes, but he does not seem to have landed there.

On the approach by sea, Ryde presents an attractive aspect, displayed as it is upon a hillside, with its steeply sloping streets, its conspicuous spires, and its fringe of handsome villas embowered in rich woods that enclose the town on either side. The most prominent landmark is the far-seen steeple of the parish Church in the upper part of the town, built after designs of Sir G. G. Scott, and ornamented with a fine show of modern art. Beside this stands the Town Hall, beyond which another church combines a Strawberry Hill Gothic effect, with a light colouring that at first sight suggests Oriental associations : it might do for a chapel to the Brighton Pavilion. Ryde has its fair allowance of churches and chapels of all denominations; but we need not look here for ancient dignity or picturesqueness, even the parish churches of such modern resorts as

24

NEWCHURCH—THE MOTHER CHURCH
OF RYDE

Ryde

Ryde or Ventnor having been originally chapels of ease to some now obscure metropolis inland. Georgian solidity or Early Victorian stucco are the highest notes of antiquity in this smart and cheerful town, which at the last census, taking in its outskirts, counted 18,000 inhabitants.

Church architecture, it may be said, is not the strongest point of the Island; though several of its churches have interesting remnants of Norman work; and I have heard of one native claiming for his parish steeple an unrecorded antiquity of more than 1600 years, in proof of which he showed the figures 1620 still legible on the fabric. One of the most notable ecclesiastical antiquities, Quarr Abbey, lies a pleasant couple of miles' walk westward from Ryde. The way is by the adjoining parish of Binstead, with its modern Church preserving some fragments of the old one, originally built by the Abbot of Quarr, "because he would not have all his tenants and the inhabitants of Binstead come to trouble the Abbey Church." A gravelled path and a lovers' lane through a series of oak copses, giving peeps of the mainland coast, bring one in view of Quarr Abbey, whose ivied ruins are now to be restored. The name Quarr or Quarraria is said to come from the Binstead quarries of Upper Eocene limestone, that figures largely in Winchester Cathedral. The abbey was founded in the middle of the twelfth century by Baldwin de Redvers, in fulfilment of a vow made during his banishment for taking Maud's part against

Stephen, after which his head was lifted up again, so that he became Lord of the Island and Earl of Devon. He was the first to be buried here, as later were other persons of note, among them the Lady Cicely, second daughter of Edward IV., who had married a gentleman of the Island. Among the numerous traditions attached to the abbey, there is one that connects a wood called Eleanor's Grove with the queen of Henry II., said to have been imprisoned here.

This was the second Cistercian house established in England, which before long absorbed so much of the Island, that the Abbot of Quarr became a petty prince. "Happy was that gentleman that could get his son to attend upon him," says Oglander: such offices as treasurer, steward, chief butler, and rent-gatherer of the abbey being sought by the cadets of the chief families. But after the Dissolution it soon fell into decay, monuments and all being sold; and in the beginning of the seventeenth century, Sir John Oglander found that the very site of the church had already been forgotten by old men, even by one who remembered the days of its glory. At this time it had been bought for £3000 by Mr Fleming, descendant of the Dutch mason brought over from the Low Country by the founder to carry out the work. "Such," moralises the knight, "is the inconstancy of Fortune, which, with the aid of her servant Time, pulleth down great things and setteth up poor things."

Ryde

Since then, the outlines have been more carefully uncovered, or traced, including part of a wall with which, by license of Edward III., this abbey was fortified against the attacks of sea-rovers, and of the French invaders who often assailed the Island. Among the old monuments recorded by Oglander was one to a "great Monsieur of France" slain here in Richard II.'s reign. The structure, of which some interesting fragments remain, was in part adapted as farm buildings, the refectory turned into a barn. But Quarr has now been bought by the community of French Benedictines that some years ago crossed the Channel to Appuldurcombe on the southern downs of the Island; and it is understood that they propose to restore the abbey as a congenial home. A swarm of nuns of the same Order has lately settled at Ryde, after a temporary residence at Northwood, near Cowes. Carisbrooke houses other foreign *religieux*, who have also a school at Ventnor. Thus the whirligig of time brings about its revenges, heretic England giving sanctuary to the churchmen of Catholic France.

From Quarr Abbey, one can stroll on to Fishbourne at the mouth of a creek called the Wootton River, which, a mile or so up, at Wootton Bridge is crossed by the road from Ryde to Cowes, passing presently behind the grounds of Osborne. Wootton is another of the oldest Wight churches, still preserving some features of the time when it was built by one of the Lisle family (*De l'Ile*) who took their name from this Island, and gave it to Dame Alice Lisle, the victim of Judge Jeffrey's bloody assize. Holding on up the wooded bottom of Wootton River, one reaches the village of Haven Street, from which an hour's walk leads back to the southern outskirts of Ryde, where all but the name of St John's Park is now overspread by brick and stone. The way by road gives a fair notion of the Island scenery on this side; and might be very pleasantly extended by lanes and field-paths, copses and commons, seaming and roughening the three mile belt between the sea and the Chalk Downs to the south.

But the many rambles that may be taken hereabouts are the business of guide-books; and the high-roads leading out of Ryde need not be pointed out to its crews of coach excursionists, and to passengers on the motor omnibuses that start here for different parts of the Island, some faring as far as Shanklin and Blackgang Chine. For the present let us leave roads and railways, to stroll along the shore to Seaview, which, at the north-eastern corner, makes a sort of chapel of ease to Ryde, as Paignton to Torquay or Westgate to Margate.

This gives another very pleasant hour's walk, to be taken along the sea-wall that continues Ryde's Esplanade. On the land side the way is much shut in by park woods and castellated villas, but it has an open view over the Solent, across which at night gleam the myriad lights of Portsmouth and Southsea; daylight shows this strait enlivened by all kinds of

shipping, and often glorified by the spectacle of a
British fleet, as sometimes by international naval
encounters in peace and courtesy. Our modern ships
of war may make a more impressive display, yet no
longer such a picturesque one as when a century
ago one visitor could tell how he saw the whole
Channel filled by a convoy, several hundreds strong,
so that "the blue waters in the distance were almost
hidden by the snow-white cloud of sails." The
pictorial place of these sails, indeed, is often taken
by the racing yachts, which run all to sail ; and "a
sail is one of the most beautiful things which man
ever invented!" So exclaims Mr George A. B.
Dewar, whose "Pageant of the Sea" papers in the
Saturday Review give us Turneresque pictures of
this landlocked waterway :—

In autumn the sea and landscapes of the Isle of Wight, towards
evening and in very still weather, seem to belong to some enchanted
country. The hills of the Island, seen from the water, grow utterly
unsubstantial then. They turn dove-coloured, and so soft and light
in their appearance that they might, to a stranger to the place, pass
for clouds on the horizon. The sea, with the mild sun on it, is
emerald ; and the band of colour that adjoins it to the north, given by
the wooded shores of Hamble and Southampton Water, is a splendid
purple. At other times, on an autumn evening like this, but with
some imperceptible difference in the atmosphere, the faint outlines of
hills far beyond Portsmouth and its land forts, have the peculiar appearance of being partly covered with a thin coating of stained snow.
Every shade of blue and green touches these waters between mainland
and island in early autumn as in summer, often changing with a
changing sky from minute to minute. . . . Not all the illusions of this
sea are kept for the hush of sundown and the shade of coming night.
The sea blooms of the Solent, films and hazes, at all seasons glorify
and mystify every ship they touch, clumsy coal barge, harbour-dredger,
graceful racing yacht.

Isle of Wight

More than half-way on our path starts up Puck-pool or Spring Vale, a row of seaside lodgings nestling under the protection of a fort that makes a link in Portsmouth's fortified *enceinte*. Here the shallow shore spreads at low water a wide stretch of sand, so firm that horses as well as children can disport themselves upon it; and it seems as if the nearest fort could almost be reached on wheels. The path holds on by a strip of meadowland; and thus we come to Seaview, that has overlaid the old name of Nettlestone Point.

Seaview, indeed, was first Seagrove before it became a flourishing family bathing-place, with the unusual setting of woods so close down to the water's edge that one may lie in a boat and hear the nightingale almost overhead; but these groves tantalise the landlubber by a crop of forbidding notices to trespassers. It has a chain pier of its own, and a regular service of steamboats from South-sea, that run on to Bembridge. This pier, with the hotel behind, splits the place into two separate sections, marked by their architecture as belonging to different strata of pleasure-seeking. The part nearer Ryde is the true old Seaview of wandering rows, bow-windowed lodging-houses, and modest refreshment rooms. On the east side of the bay has sprung up a newer, smarter, redder bit of esplanade, making a pretty contrast to its dark green background. A private road leads to this end, which, else, at high tide is cut off, so that the butcher or greengrocer may be seen delivering his wares by boat in quite Venetian manner. There are sands for children, and rocks for scrambling, and a shallow beach for launching canoes on these safe waters, where the red sails of the Bembridge Yacht Club make dots of colour, as do the tents here taking the place of bathing-machines. Another peculiar feature is the diving-boards anchored out at sea, since the tide, creeping up to the Esplanade garden gates, woos paddlers rather than swimmers. Seaview, in short, holds itself something out of the common in the way of bathing-places, dealing with strangers rather in the wholesale way of house-letting than the retail trade of apartments.

Beyond the broken point, where one seems to catch Nature in her workshop, kneading clay into firmer forms, a rough walk along the shore of Priory Bay leads on to St Helen's, reached inland by the road through Nettlestone Green. Once clear of houses, we plunge among the rank greenery of the Island, too much monopolised here by the grounds of the Priory, which preserves the name of a colony of monks swarmed over from France to St Helen's in early Plantagenet days. This was one of the properties bought by Emmanuel Badd, who, *teste* Sir John Oglander, began life as a poor shoemaker's apprentice at Newport, "but by God's blessinge and ye loss of 5 wyfes, he grewe very ritch," rose to be High Sheriff of

Isle of Wight

Hants, and was buried under an epitaph in Jacobean
taste, ending

> So good a Bad doth this same grave contain,
> Would all like Bad were that with us remain !

But at St Helen's we have rounded the corner of
the Island, which we may now survey from another
line of operations.

NEWPORT

BEFORE holding on by road, rail, or boat along the coast, let us take a course through the centre of the Island, on which we can pay due respect to its capital. From Ryde, Cowes, and Freshwater run railways that meet at Newport, where the Medina begins to be navigable, and thence go off branches to Ventnor and Sandown. This junction, then, makes the radiating point of the Isle of Wight's communications; and all its main roads converge at Newport, which, though not quite so large as Ryde, and not so well recruited by strangers, is a flourishing place of over 10,000 people.

One sees at once that this is no *ville de plaisance*, but the home of all sorts and conditions of men, taking toll on the country round by varied industry. Roman origin has been claimed for it on hint of the straight streets and crossings that give it a more regular aspect than most country towns, shading off indeed on the skirts into wandering lanes and rising outgrowths of the "Mount Pleasant" order. A peculiar feature is the little Quay quarter, where the Lugley stream from Carisbrooke comes in to make the Medina navigable for small vessels freighted with timber, coals, malt, wheat, and so forth. But the tidal river below Newport adorns the landscape only at high water, being too often a broad ribbon of slime creeping between low banks, not beautified by the big cement works lower down, that get their raw material in mud as well as chalk. More picturesque are the Chalk Downs, on the other side embracing the town with their green shoulders and quarried faces.

The central cross-way is marked by a memorial to Queen Victoria. Close by, too narrowly shut up in its square, stands St Thomas's Church, whose stately tower and high roof pitch makes the boss of Newport from all points of view. This is little more than half a century old, taking the place of the ancient shrine dedicated to the memory of St Thomas à Becket, which was rather unwarrantably pulled down, that "holy blissful martyr's" dedication being at the same time usurped by Thomas the Apostle, a saint more congenial to our age. Some of its old treasures are preserved in the present structure, notably the Charles I. pulpit, carved with personifications of Justice and Mercy, the Three Graces, the Four Cardinal Virtues, and the Seven Liberal Arts, among which a goat marks the name of the artist, Thomas Caper. Another antiquity is the monument to Sir Edward Horsey, Captain of the Island, 1565-82, showing his canopied effigy in armour with an epitaph attributing to him, after the manner of such, more virtues than he gets credit for in history. The

NEWPORT

most beautiful monument is a modern one by Baron
Marochetti, to commemorate Princess Elizabeth,
Charles I.'s deformed and sickly daughter, buried in
the old church 1650; but her tomb had been forgotten
till the accidental discovery of the coffin in 1793.
She is represented as found dead by her attendants,
according to tradition, with her face resting on the
pages of an open Bible, the gift of her father; and a
happy touch of symbolism shows the iron bars of her
life broken by death. Along with this monument,
Queen Victoria contributed two memorial windows
and a medallion of the Prince Consort by the same
sculptor.

There is no room for a churchyard in St Thomas's
Square; but across South Street will be found the
old cemetery, close packed with graves. One, seen
from the path leading along it, hints at a story too
common a century ago, an ugly obelisk to the
memory of Valentine Gray, "the little sweep," erected
by public subscription "in testimony of the general
feeling for suffering innocence." Here is buried
John Hamilton Reynolds, Keats' friend, and Hood's
brother-in-law, who himself in youth bid fair to earn
poetic fame. He is understood to be part author of
Hood's *Odes to Great People;* and he was to have
collaborated with Keats in a volume of Italian tales,
not to speak of work of his own like "a runaway
ring at Wordsworth's Peter Bell"; but after penning
stanzas not unsuccessfully, he had the singular fate
of taking to engrossing as a solicitor. He seems to

have grown soured or sottish in his later life, which
he ended obscurely as an official of the Newport
County Court.

Of the few old buildings left in Newport, the most
remarkable is the Jacobean Grammar School at the
corner of Lugley Street and the road going down to
cross Towngate bridge for Parkhurst and West
Cowes. The old portion, for a later addition has
been made, is interesting not only in itself, but as
understood to have housed Charles I. during his last
abortive negotiations with the Parliament, at the end
of which the king was hurried away to his doom.
Here, at that day, it was usual to receive captains
and other great men coming into the Island, with an
oration prepared by the schoolmaster and recited by
a promising pupil; but one fears that on his later
appearances at Newport poor Charles was somewhat
scrimply treated in the way of loyal addresses.

Visitors to Newport nowadays come mainly for
the sake of Carisbrooke Castle, which is perhaps the
chief attraction of the Island, drawing thousands of
excursionists on a holiday occasion. Carisbrooke, at
one time overshadowing the humble beginnings of
Newport, is now almost one of its suburbs, the
distance being only a mile or so. From the end of
High Street, the way is by the Mall, a dignified
parade that suggests Bath or Clifton. The road
divides at a memorial cross to Sir John Simeon,
Tennyson's friend and neighbour at Swainston,
notable as the first Catholic to sit in a modern

parliament, though he belonged to a family whose theological associations were expressed by the Simeon Trust for stocking pulpits with Evangelical divines. Either fork leads to Carisbrooke, that to the right being the highway for the village, and the other going more directly to the castle, under a height on which is the cemetery.

The Windsor of Newport is in itself a place to delight our American guests, a long, steep village street of true British irregularity, giving off straggling lanes of rose-wreathed cottages, through which, in the hollow, flows a clear and shallow brook, bordered by luxuriant hedges, and by notices of "Teas Provided." The main thoroughfare, mounting up to the Church, shows an unusual number of hotels and other places of entertainment; and the excursion vehicles that rendezvous here in summer rather disturb the peaceful charm of Carisbrooke, which too evidently lives on its visitors.

What is left of the Church, originally a double one divided between the parish and a priory that stood here, still makes a spacious structure, rearing the best tower in the Island, and enshrining some monuments and relics, most notable among them the tomb of Sir Nicholas Wadham's wife, two generations before the founder of Wadham College. A quaint wooden tablet recalls the career of William Keeling, one of the earliest of our East Indian officials, whose name is preserved by the Keeling or Cocos Islands discovered by him far out in the Indian Ocean, in our time to be occupied by a Scottish family named Ross, who made this atoll group into a thriving settlement. The churchyard has a good show of old tombstones, including a weeping willow, railed in, as fanciful memorial of a former vicar.

A late incumbent was the Rev. E. Boucher James, whose Archæological and Historical Letters made valuable contributions to the annals of the Island. He does not omit to dig up the buried renown of his predecessor, the Rev. Alexander Ross, that erudite and voluminous Scot, now remembered only by the luck of rhyme that made a "sage philosopher" to have "read Alexander Ross over," yet by his pen or his preaching, or somehow, he seems to have gained a considerable fortune, part of which he left to the poor of Carisbrooke. Any modern reader who cares to tackle this once-esteemed author, might try a spell at his "Πανσεβεια: View of all Religions," which is still to be seen at libraries, if not on railway book-stalls. Another Carisbrooke worthy commemorated by Mr James was William Stephens, who, after losing his fortune and his seat as member for Newport, took part in General Oglethorpe's philanthropic plan for settling Georgia, came to be president of the colony, and ended his life rather miserably in squabbles with the disciples of Whitfield and other discontented immigrants. Among this learned parson's records is the pretty story of Dorothy Osborne, who, travelling with her father and brother in the days of the Civil War, at an inn hereabouts fell in with the future Sir William Temple, and the beginning of their courtship was through one of the young men scrawling on the window some disrespectful words about the Parliament, which led to the whole party being haled before the governor, to be released when Dorothy took the offence on herself: those stern Ironsides did not war against ladies. More than once the late vicar has to speak of his "friend and parishioner," Henry Morley, who here ended the labours on English literature that made his name well known both in England and America.

Beside the parsonage is a sixpenny show of pavements, and other remains of a Roman villa unearthed about half a century ago, but since thrown into the shade by the larger one discovered at Brading. A more recent sign of Roman invasion is the establishment here of foreign religious communities, driven by French secularism into this pleasant exile. It is no common village that clusters about the tower, looking down "from its centuries of grey calm on the fitful stir and fret around it, and the fevered hopes and fears that must end at last in the quiet green mounds at its feet."

The Castle stands across the valley, where its grey walls, buoyed by a flagstaff, hardly peep out above the wooded slopes and the thick greenery that floods the moat. This most picturesquely situated pile represents a very ancient fortress, held by the Romans, as by ruder warriors before them, then expanded and strengthened according to the needs

of different times, so as now in its half-dilapidated,
half-restored state, to form a charming medley of
ruinous repair, wreathed with various historic
memories, and specially haunted by those of the
last year in which its walls were sternly guarded.

The oldest part is the Norman Keep, raised upon
a mound that gives a fine prospect over Newport
and down the Medina. Beautiful views can also
be had from the moated walls within which Carisbrooke's inner defences were enclosed by an Italian
engineer in the days of the Armada. His work
appears to have been stopped by the failure of that
enterprise; had it been completed after his designs,
this would have made the strongest fortress in
Elizabethan England; and it enjoys the distinction
of a virgin stronghold with no record of capture,
unless may be counted to the contrary its honourable
surrender by Lady Portland's tiny garrison to the
Parliamentary forces. The outer entrance bears
the date 1598. The massive inner Gate-house,
begun at the same time as the Keep, shows work
of different periods, including recent restoration.
Here, as so often in the Island, something has to
be paid for admission; and there are further small
charges for what an irreverent mind might term the
side-shows. The main attraction is the remains of
the royal prison that gives this castle its special
interest as scene of almost the latest English
romance in the history of such "grey and ivied
walls where ruin greenly dwells." Its earliest note

CARISBROOKE CASTLE

in more misty annals seems to be that here Sir Bevis of Hampton, having overcome his wicked stepfather, Sir Murdour, caused that traitor to be boiled to death in a caldron of pitch and brimstone, one of the facts not now known to "every school-boy." But such a well-informed personage is no doubt aware how the most famous event of this castle's story was King Charles' confinement here.

After his escape from Hampton Court in November 1647, attended by three gentlemen, the king made for the Solent, and crossed to the Isle of Wight, believing the Governor, Colonel Hammond, to be favourable to him. But Hammond, a connection of Cromwell, and son-in-law of John Hampden, received Charles as a prisoner rather than a sovereign,—at first, indeed, treated with respect and allowed to ride out hunting about Parkhurst Forest, with the governor in his train. Carisbrooke was so slightly guarded, that the king judged it easy to escape when he pleased. At the end of the year, he did propose to escape to Southampton down the Medina, but found himself baffled by a change of wind to the north. After that, he was kept in closer restraint, most of his faithful attendants being dismissed, and the Castle made a real prison. One Captain Burley tried to raise a rescue for him at Newport, but was taken prisoner, to be with legal mockery tried and executed for treason against the king in his parliament.

Poor Charles was soon stripped of what royal

ceremonial had been left him. For exercise he walked up and down the Tilt Yard turned into a bowling-green, or round the ramparts, looking sadly out on the green slopes that bounded his view. He spent much time in reading, writing, and gloomy meditation. Now, according to a discredited tradition, he finished that *Eikon Basilike* which has been almost conclusively shown to be the work of Dr Thomas Gauden. Nor should his admirers press a dubious title for him as poet, in the verses entitled *Majesty in Misery*, that begin by a rather lame invocation—

> Great Monarch of the world, from whose power springs
> The potency and power of kings,
> Record the royal woe my suffering brings,
>
> And teach my tongue that ever did confine
> Its faculties in truth's seraphic line,
> To track the treasons of Thy foes and mine.

As sympathising attendants he had Harrington, author of *Oceana*, and Thomas Herbert, who stuck by him to the end; while one Osborne, put near him as a spy for the Parliament, seems to have been so far won by the captive's woes, that he is found helping an attempt at escape. The most authentic occupation for the king's too much leisure was intriguing with his friends, by means of letters in cipher and other communications through the trusty servants left him, till this secret correspondence was tapped by his custodians.

His cause was not yet lost. While Cromwell

Newport

strove to trim the captainless ship of State between the extreme Presbyterians and Levellers, there were signs of reaction in the king's favour. Fresh civil war broke out from the still smouldering embers in different parts. Hamilton with his army of Scots invaded England. Prince Charles with a loyal section of the fleet hovered upon the east coast from his base in Holland; and it seems strange that he made no attempt to rescue his father by a landing on the Island, even when Parliamentary ships guarded the Solent. The queen, on the continent, was hatching war against the distracted government *de facto*, which had good reason for holding her husband fast, lest he should place himself at the head of any of these movements.

In March a plot had nearly succeeded, by which Charles should have broken out and ridden away with a band of loyal gentlemen of the Island, as Mary did from Loch Leven. But he was not so lucky as his bewitching grandmother. He stuck fast in a barred window, and had to give up the attempt. Two months later, the bar having been filed or eaten away with acid, he tried again, but being more closely watched, found Hammond on the alert and double guards posted on the walls. Now confined in closer quarters, the king seems to have lost heart. His uncrowned head turned grey, he let his beard grow, and the once trim cavalier became careless of his dress. Nor had his gaoler Hammond a happy time of it, who is found complaining to

Isle of Wight

Cromwell of the "sad and heavy burden" laid upon him, when he had hoped for peace and quiet in retiring from active service to this backwater of civil strife.

Yet still Charles might have been saved by a little more of the craft that had brought him to ruin. In September he was moved to Newport for a last effort at negotiation between himself and the Parliament, which now saw reason to dread the army as a more formidable tyrant. But hopes of an understanding stuck upon the point of religion, the "conscientious and untrustworthy" king proving firm in his devotion to prelacy. He once again seems to have thought of escaping, in spite of having given his word to remain at Newport. Then, while the treaty dragged itself on, the soldiers, exasperated by renewed bloodshed, raised a cry for sharper measures. Cromwell began to talk loudly of justice. A band of his troopers appeared in the Island to "guard" the residence of Charles, who now refused to escape, as bound by his parole. On the last night of November, the shifty and irresolute king was forcibly carried off to Yarmouth by two troops of horse, to be ferried across to Hurst Castle, and thence, before Christmas, taken to Windsor as prisoner of the army, that meanwhile, by "Pride's Purge," had got rid of the moderate party in Parliament, putting England under martial law.

After Charles' execution, Carisbrooke received two more royal prisoners, Princess Elizabeth and the little Duke of Gloucester, kept in hand as possible figure-head of a constitutional monarchy, now that his two elder brothers were out of the Common-wealth's power. The treatment of these young captives makes a pleasant contrast to the fate of Louis XVI.'s children in their harsh prison, though some extremists had proposed that the young malig-nants should be "apprenticed to honest trades." A yearly £1000 was granted for their support, £5000 having been the king's allowance. But almost at once the poor princess caught cold through getting wet at a game of bowls, and a month later was laid, as we saw, in Newport Church. The little duke, addressed as "Master Harry," was kept here for two years, then allowed by the Protector to join his family on the continent, England being by this time provided with a ruler who made more than a figure-head. This young prince died of small-pox, just as the Restoration was opening brighter prospects for his house. A later captive at Carisbrooke was Sir Henry Vane, a man too good for those troubled times, whose fate was to offend all parties, driven out of his governorship in Massachusetts, imprisoned by Cromwell, and executed under Charles II. Sir William Davenant is said also to have spent part of his imprisonment here.

The scenes traditionally connected with that moving story are shown to visitors. Relics of the unfortunate Charles and his family are preserved in a museum above the gateway, a part of the castle restored by way of memorial to her husband by

Princess Henry of Battenburg, who, as Governor of the Island, is *châtelaine*, her deputy occupying a habitable portion as keeper. The ruined chapel of St Nicholas in the courtyard has also been restored, in memory of the king whom modern historians make not so much of a saint and a martyr. Another sight of the Castle is its deep well, from which water is drawn by a wheel worked by a dynasty of donkeys that have the reputation of enjoying longer life than falls to the lot of most monarchs.

Carisbrooke has a station, a little to the north, on the Freshwater line. Beyond this, the westward high-road is edged by a front of dark firs that mark the enclosure of Parkhurst or Carisbrooke Forest, compact fragment of a once more extensive woodland, swelling up into eminences of two or three hundred feet. This is Government property, but ways through it are open for shady rambles, very pleasant on a hot day. A field-path from Newport, starting by a foot-bridge beside a prominent block of brewery buildings just below the station, leads to the south-east corner of the forest, where workhouse, prison, and barracks adjoin one another to make up a little town. Parkhurst Prison, whose inmates one has seen engaged in the idyllic occupation of haymaking within a fence of fixed bayonets, ranks as a sort of sanatorium among our convict depôts, to which delicate criminals are sent rather than to the bleak heights of Portland or Dartmoor.

The soldiers at the barracks are kept in better

order than that Scots regiment that proved such a
curse and corruption to the quiet Wight parishes in
Oglander's time. He represents them as billeted in
the Island "because they should not run away, being
constrained for the most part to serve contrary to
their wills"—*volunteers*, as he elsewhere calls them
—"a proud, beggarly nation, and I hope we shall
never be troubled with the like [again], especially the
red-shanks, or the Highlanders, being as barbarous
in nature as their clothes." These strangers, "insolent
by reason of their unanimous holding together,"
brought about so many "inconveniences," murders,
rapes, robberies, and so forth, that when at length
they were shipped off to the siege of La Rochelle,
after being reviewed by Charles on Arreton Down,
the worthy knight can record how "we were free
from our Egyptian thraldom, or like Spain from the
Moors, for since the Danish slavery never were these
Islanders so oppressed." In the outspoken fashion
of his day, he notes how the Scots left behind them a
considerable strain of northern blood, which may
have been not altogether an evil for a too closely
connected neighbourhood, where, if all tales are true,
marrying in and in has generated a good deal of
physical and mental feebleness.

Keats, who seems to have written part of
Endymion at Carisbrooke, denounces the barracks
at Parkhurst as a "nest of debauchery." But at the
worst, they may have been an Arcadian nook compared to that East India Company's recruits depôt

near Ryde, described by Scott, in *The Surgeon's Daughter*, as a gaol of adventurous scum of society swept together by crimps and kidnappers. Sir Walter must have visited or at least coasted "the shore of that beautiful island, which he who once sees never forgets," when in 1807 he stayed with his friend Stewart Rose at Gundimore on the Hampshire coast. Since his day, the Island has seen various samples of Highland soldiers, and found them not too barbarous either in dress or manners.

By Parkhurst there is a pleasant way to Gurnard Bay, the nearest bathing-place on the coast. Cowes, under half a dozen miles off, may be gained by roads on either side the river, or by boat when the tide serves. The well-shod and wary explorer might trace the Medina upwards through the Downs, and among the peaty bogs of the "Wilderness" on to its obscure source behind the Undercliff. On either side the "quarried downs of Wight" offer fine airy walks with valley villages for goal, or such points as the ancient British settlement, whose pit dwellings may be traced by an antiquary's eye in the hollow below Rowborough Downs, near the road leading south from Carisbrooke. On the other side of the Medina, by St George's Down, is mounted the ridge of chalk stretching to Brading and Bembridge.

In fact Newport, too much neglected by tourists, unless as a halting-place, would make an excellent station for visiting the whole Island. I must be content with taking the reader on by the central railway to the Undercliff. This goes out from Newport with the line to Sandown, threading the Downs into the Yar Valley; then at Merston Junction it turns off towards the southern heights swelling up beyond Godshill station. But one must not forget to mention Shide, on the outskirts of Newport, not only as a station for its golf-links on Pan Down, but as a spot in wider touch with the world than any other on the Island, for here Dr John Milne, F.R.S., has his Seismological Observatory, if that be a fit title for an installation of instruments by which earthquakes, thousands of miles away, are recorded long before they get into newspapers—some indeed that never get into further notice, spending their force at the bottom of the sea or in wildernesses beyond the ken of "our own correspondent."

Godshill is one of the prettiest of the Island villages, claiming its name from that oft-told legend of supernatural interference with the building of a church, which by miraculous power was moved to its present site on an eminence, where it holds up its tower as a conspicuous landmark. This church is often visited both for the prospect from it, and for its architectural merits and interesting memorials. Besides a sixteenth century altar tomb of Sir John Leigh and monuments of the Worsley family, it contains a specimen of their once famous art collection in a picture of *Daniel in the Lion's Den*, said to be in part by Rubens, or at least after his style. An older patron is recorded by a tablet praising one of the benefactors of the Newport Grammar School.

> Here lies the mortal part of Richard Gard,
> While his freed spirit meets with heaven's reward ;
> His gifts endowed the schools, the needy raised
> And by the latest memory will be praised.
> And may our Isle be filled with such a name,
> And be like him whom virtue clothed with fame ;
> Blessed with the poor, the scholars too were blest
> Through such a donor that is gone to rest.

A strange commentary on the truthfulness of epitaphs is the account of that late lamented given by his contemporary Oglander, declaring him the knavish son of a French refugee, whose father, Pierre Garde, had been executed for treason in his own country. An extract on this head makes a good specimen of Sir John's random jottings, that open such curious peeps into the state of his native Island at that date. One takes the liberty of correcting his spelling ; but the style seems past mending.

Richard, the father, was a notable sly fellow, dishonest and given to filching ; he brought some tricks out of France with him. *Vide*— he would steal a cow, and putting a loaf of bread hot out of the oven on her horns, make her horns so supple that they would turn any way he pleased, so as to disfigure the beast that the owner might not know her again. Many other shifts he had, being a man of no great conscience, by which means he recovered some wealth, and died. His sons, Richard and Peter, did not degenerate ; Richard was as crafty a knave as any (except his brother) in a whole country ; he was good at reading and understanding of old evidences, whereby he got many into his hands, and so forced the owners to a composition. He was indifferently skilled in law, a most penurious base fellow, and of little religion ; he died about 1616, and in his will gave Richard, the eldest son of Peter, the better part of his estate, having no children of his

GODSHILL

own. He willed his body to be coffined in lead, and to be laid but 2 foot deep in the earth, in the porch of Godshill Church, as unwilling that too much earth should hinder him from rising at the resurrection ; where we will leave him, to speak of Peter, the second brother, and son of Richard the Bandit.

This Peter had left him by his father a little land at St Helens (which how it might be purchased in his own name, being an alien, I leave) worth per annum £5. Richard the elder brother being willing to cheat his brother Peter of the land, was an importunate suitor to buy it of him ; the other, as crafty, permitted him to feed him with money, and having had half or better of the worth of it, was drawn (as he made himself very unwilling) to sign a deed of sale thereof to his brother ; but he being at that time under age ; the first act he did when he came of age was to cheat the cheater, and nullify that deed by non-age. The enmity then between the two brothers was great ; they vilified one another, and discovered each other's knavery to the view of the whole Island. I cannot omit one in silence, being so notorious. Richard Garde had good store of monies, and durst not trust any man with it, no not his own house, but hid it in a pot underground in the field, where one Smyth, his neighbour, mistrusting some such matter, observed him more narrowly, and by watching him found an opportunity to gain the hidden pot. The other when he missed it, esteeming it little less than his God, had well-near hanged himself, but that he had some confidence by the devil's means to recover it, whereupon the brothers, now friends, consult of the means—Peter as the more active man undertakes it, goes to a witch near Kingwood, or somewhere, and brought home certain hope of the short return of the monies ; whereupon this Smyth, the Saturday following, was taken on Hazely Hill on his return from Newport, and there in a great storm was beaten, haled, whipped, misused, and almost killed (had not some the next morning found him by chance) not knowing or seeing who did act it, but affirmed it was the devil ; and being long ill after, could not be quiet in conscience till he had brought home the pot of silver again to Richard Garde's house to Binstead, according to the true relation formerly made to Peter by the witch. Peter, he got still lands and livings, whether by right or wrong I suppose he little respected ; he was, and is, one of the slyest, craftiest knaves that I know ; wit and judgment in matters of law he hath enough both to serve his own turn and to cozen his neighbours ; a man worse spoken of I never knew.

Isle of Wight

A more honourable name was the Worsleys, here commemorated, long one of the chief families in the Island, that had its principal seat at Appuldurcombe on the high downs above Godshill. Its most notable member was Sir Richard Worsley, a cultured Georgian squire, who wrote the history of the Island in quarto, and on his travels made a celebrated art collection to adorn the stately classical mansion which he completed, replacing what had been a Benedictine Abbey. By marriage, the house and its treasures passed to the Earls of Yarborough, who, half a century ago left the Island, carrying away the art collection to be mainly dispersed.

The Lord Yarborough of early Victorian times was a "character," doughty commodore of the R.Y.S., who tried to play Canute against the advance of railways, a prejudice then shared by high and low, as we learn in Herbert Spencer's autobiography. His arbitrary lordship had his lands protected against this radical innovation by a guard charged to take into custody anybody with a theodolite, or who looked in the least like a railway engineer. Upon one occasion, a man newly appointed to the post, meeting his master in a secluded part of the estate, at once collared him, an incident to be paralleled by Mr John Mytton's famous fight, in the disguise of a sweep, with his own keeper.

The mansion, whose name should be strongly accented on the last syllable, stands in a combe, well displayed against its background of dark wood.

52

Newport

Since it passed to "overners," it has been turned into an hotel, then into a school; and a few years ago was acquired by a community of Benedictine monks exiled from France, thus coming back to its original owners. As already mentioned, this Order has since acquired Quarr Abbey, and are spreading their establishments so fast over the Island, that sound Protestants dread to see given up to cloisters all of it that is not dedicated to golf.

For laymen and strangers in general the most interesting spot of this demesne is the Worsley obelisk on the highest point of the Downs, raised by Sir Richard Worsley to a height of 70 feet, but in 1831 struck by lightning that shattered its huge blocks of granite into wild confusion. From this half-ruined landmark the most extensive view in the Island displays its whole length and breadth, from the chalk cliffs of Culver to those about the Needles.

The railway, whose whistle might make that prejudiced Lord Yarborough turn in his grave, of course keeps clear of far prospects, taking a break in the Downs to thread its way through by Whitwell, which has a remarkable restored church, originally composed of two chapels, one belonging to Gatcombe, some miles north-west, once seat of another branch of the Worsley family, and having an ancient church of its own. Thus the line drops down into the rich greenery of the Undercliff, at St Lawrence turning eastward above the shore, to reach Ventnor beside Steephill Castle.

THE EAST SIDE

THE more direct route from Ryde to Ventnor is by road, rail, or boat along the east coast. From the Newport line diverges the old Ventnor railway, at Brading sending off a branchlet for Bembridge, then holding on behind Sandown and Shanklin. Thus on this side are strung together the oldest and one of the youngest settlements of the Isle of Wight.

Brading, an hour's walk from Ryde, seems an insignificant place now; but it claims to have been the ancient metropolis of the Island in days when St Helens was its chief port. Brading Harbour, still a tidal creek that at high water dignifies the landscape, once made a wider and deeper gulf, which guide-books of a century back describe as an inland lake set in woods. Time was, says Sir John Oglander, that boats came up to the middle of Brading Street, and in the haven below there would be choice of twenty good shipmasters to undertake any voyage. Then the harbour having become choked by unwholesome marshes, an attempt was made to embank them, in which work Sir Hugh Middleton of New River fame had a hand, and

certain "ignorant Dutchmen" were brought over
to put in practice the art to which they owed their
own native soil. But the Dutchmen's dykes broke
down; and the land was not thoroughly reclaimed
till our own time saw the enterprise accomplished
by that "Liberator" Company of else evil renown.

Thus Brading came to be gradually stranded
some mile or two inland. The townlet, that once
sent two members to Parliament, has relics to show
of its old dignity, its bull ring, its stocks, and its
Norman Church, rich in monuments, notably the
Oglander Chapel enshrining tombs of a family settled
at Nunwell on Brading Down for many centuries,
among them the effigy of that Sir John Oglander,
whose memoranda have been so much drawn on by
later writers. He tells how then "many score" of
Oglanders lay in this oldest church of the Island,
where the latest addition to the family chapel is a
fine monument to his descendant of the Victorian
age.

The churchyard contains more than one celebrated epitaph, such as that set to music by Dr
Calcott—

Forgive, blest shade, the tributary tear !

and another on a child—

This lovely bud, so young, so fair,
Called hence by early doom,
Just came to show how sweet a flower
In Paradise would bloom.

Here was buried "Jane the young Cottager," whose
humble name has been spread far by Legh Rich-

mond, curate of this parish at the end of the eighteenth century. It is to be feared that his writings are not so well known to our generation as they once were in the religious world, for he belonged to that school of Evangelical saints, who dwelt more on "Gospel truths" than on "sound Church feeling"; and his long-spun death-bed scenes are hardly to the taste of readers who have learned to look for more piquant flavours in the literature of edification. But in the Isle of Wight, where Protestantism puts down its foot the more firmly for recent Catholic invasion, this kindly pastor's "Annals of the Poor" still seem to find a sale, as they once did in many languages. Mr Boucher James goes so far as to say that "in a small way Legh Richmond did for the Isle of Wight what Walter Scott did for the Scottish Highlands," by drawing tourists to seek out the scenes of his tracts. At all events he deserves the brass now placed to his memory in Brading Church.[1]

The much restored Church claims to represent that first erected on the same site by Wilfred, apostle of the Island. But another lion of Brading is older than its church, though unknown to Legh Rich-

[1] The *Errata* volume of the D.N.B. does penance for a curious slip in its account of this half-forgotten worthy, where the Shepherd's Bush Public Library is stated to be a joint-memorial to him and to Charles Keene. I was so struck by this odd conjunction of patron saints, that I made a pilgrimage of veridification to their reputed shrine, and found it was *Leigh Hunt's* memory that has been not so unequally yoked together with the *Punch* artist's.

mond's generation. This is the Roman villa, discovered a generation ago by Mr Hilton Price,
Director of the Society of Antiquaries, which boasts
itself to be the finest of such miniature Pompeiis
in England. It stands about a mile to the south-
west, near Yarbridge, the way being easily found,
since direction posts are never wanting in the Isle
of Wight where there is anything to pay for admission ; and the tarred sheds that protect the remains
stand conspicuous against a chalk cutting on the
Downs. A score or so apartments have been unearthed, in some of which were found many relics
of the Roman occupation, the most interesting part
of the show being the tesselated pavements with
their mosaic designs. There appear traces of two
successive ownerships, and of the villa having been
destroyed by fire, perhaps on the evacuation of
Britain by the Roman troops. The complete building seems to have been composed of the *Urbana*,
or master's dwelling, the *Rustica*, or quarters for
dependents, and the *Fructuaria*, store-houses and
offices, arranged on three sides of a rectangle.

From Brading the central line of downs runs
westward for half-a-dozen miles to the valley of the
Medina. On the height known as Ashey Down, a
stone pyramid, erected as a sea-mark, makes one of
the favourite view-points, looking over half the Island
and across the Solent to Portsmouth. Further along,
below a crest marked by Saxon burrows, Arreton
has a fine prospect upon the valley of the Yar to the

south. This is one of the Island's show villages, where excursion coaches stop to let their passengers see the Church with its medley of Gothic features, and the grave of the "Dairyman's Daughter," another of Legh Richmond's heroines, lying at peace among warriors and knights of old. The old manor-house of this scattered village bears marks of bygone dignity; but destruction has come upon Knighton, which a century or so back could still be called the stateliest hall of the Island.

In the *Dairyman's Daughter*, Legh Richmond turns his thoughts from heaven to earth to give a description of what one surveys from the Ashey Down sea-mark; one may omit some final features which have altered since his day, as well as the moral drawn by the good clergyman from the fact that so "much of the natural beauties of Paradise still remain in the world."

Southward the view was terminated by a long range of hills, at about six miles distance. They met, to the westward, another chain of hills, of which the one whereon I sat formed a link, and the whole together nearly encompassed a rich and fruitful valley, filled with corn-fields and pastures. Through this vale winded a small valley for many miles ; much cattle were feeding on its banks. Here and there lesser eminences arose in the valley ; some covered with wood, others with corn or grass, and a few with heath or fern. One of these little hills was distinguished by a parish church at the top, presenting a striking feature in the landscape. Another of these elevations, situated in the centre of the valley, was adorned with a venerable holly-tree, which has grown there for ages. Its singular height and wide-spreading dimensions not only render it an object of curiosity to the traveller, but of daily usefulness to the pilot, as a mark visible from the sea, whereby to direct his vessel safe into harbour. Villages,

WATER MEADOWS OF THE YAR
NEAR ALVERSTONE

churches, country-seats, farmhouses, and cottages were scattered over every part of the southern valley. . . .

South-eastward, I saw the open ocean, bounded only by the horizon. The sun shone, and gilded the waves with a glittering light that sparkled in the most brilliant manner. More to the east, in continuation of that line of hills where I was placed, rose two downs, one beyond the other; both covered with sheep, and the sea just visible over the farthest of them, as a terminating boundary. In this point, ships were seen, some sailing, others at anchor. Here the little river, which watered the southern valley, finished its course, and ran through meadows into the sea, in an eastward direction.

On the north the sea appeared like a noble river, varying from three to seven miles in breadth, between the banks of the opposite coast and those of the island which I inhabited. Immediately underneath me was a fine woody district of country, diversified by many pleasing objects. Distant towns were visible on the opposite shore. Numbers of ships occupied the sheltered station which this northern channel afforded them. The eye roamed with delight over an expanse of near and remote beauties, which alternately caught the observation, and which harmonised together, and produced a scene of peculiar interest.

Westward the hills followed each other, forming several intermediate and partial valleys, in a kind of undulations, like the waves of the sea ; and, bending to the south, completed the boundary of the larger valley before described, to the southward of the hill on which I sat.

This river Yar, not to be confounded with its namesake on the other side of the Island, rises in the southern downs that bound the prospect over its valley. At Brading, it finds a gap through the northern heights, beyond which it winds sluggishly into that shrunken harbour. Above the left side stands St Helens, with its wide green and fringe of leafy lanes, having moved up from a lower site, where an ivied fragment of the old church shows its whitewashed face to the sea as a beacon. The sandy spit here has also been turned to use for golf-links, that helped yachting to make the fortune of Bembridge. The Island seems now in a fair way of being half laid out in golf grounds, but these were the first, or among the first, which, though small, had the advantage of a mild climate to invite enthusiasts in winter, when elsewhere red balls would be necessary for their absorbing pastime. Links for ladies are a later addition, on the opposite side of the river, that the eyes of neither sex may be distracted from a foursome to what might become a twosome game of life.

Bembridge itself, linked to St Helens by a ferry boat, nestles very prettily on the wooded point opposite. The nucleus of nautically named inns and cottages is much overlaid by hotel and lodging-house accommodation, and by villas whose owners declare Bembridge to be the Island's pleasantest spot. One of its chief attractions, after golf, is the view of shipping in the Solent mouth; but it has some pretty spots on land, such as the avenue running inland from the bathing beach. To the south it is sheltered by the Foreland, the most easterly point, over which we may hold by mounting lanes, or take a rough path round the shore, tide permitting, that has also to be considered in boating about the dangerous Bembridge Ledges roughening the sea at low water.

Thus we pass on to the curve of Whitecliff Bay, where the chalk of the Downs is broken by an expanse of Eocene beds, making for the geologist a foretaste

SANDOWN BAY

of that more glowing transformation scene shown in Alum Bay at the Island's western end. The Culver Cliffs at this end are protected by a fort which has masked the Hermit's Hole, a cave once used by smugglers. On the other side of Bembridge is a small fortress, now so far behind the times that it was lately advertised as suitable for a private residence or an hotel.

Beyond Whitecliff Bay, the cliffs curve into the block of Bembridge Down, crowned by a modern fort that has usurped the originally more conspicuous site of Lord Yarborough's monument, now neighboured by a Marconi Telegraph Station. On the southern slope are the tiny Norman Church and decayed manor-house of Yaverland, which makes a scene in the *Dairyman's Daughter*. Here we have come round to Sandown Bay, the largest and openest in the Island, reached by road and rail from Brading through the gap at Yarbridge.

Sandown stands in a break of the cliffs, behind the centre of its bay, compared of course to the Bay of Naples by those who never saw Vesuvius. With its hotels, rows of smart lodging-houses, batteries of bathing-machines, esplanade, arcade, and other very modern features, this seems one of the most growing places in the Island; and I trust Sandown will not take it amiss to be described as perhaps the most commonplace resort here, or at least the most like the ordinary Saturday-to-Mondayville. Its strong point is wide, firm sands for children, and, on a common behind the town, excellent golf-links for their elders, about the height known as "Majuba Hill," the views from which are complained of by votaries as interfering with strict attention to their game. The summer season of this bathing-place is so prosperous that some day its esplanade and Shanklin's may stretch out to meet along the couple of miles of cliff walk separating them. As link between them springs up Lake, with its sumptuous "Home of Rest," and its headquarters of Isle of Wight cricket, behind the cliff descent at Littlestairs.

Sandown Pier has met with rough handling from winter waves, to which, however, the enterprising town will not give in so easily as did King Canute, whose renowned object-lesson against pride, according to legend, had its scene not far off, across the Solent. The railway station, which stands some way back from the sea, is a junction of lines to Newport, Ventnor, and Ryde, so that Sandown visitors can easily reach more picturesque corners of the Island, or can soon gain the Downs framing the green valley of the Yar. Up this valley the first station is Alverston, near a knoll known as Queen's Bower, from the tradition that upon it Isabella de Fortibus watched the chase in what was then Bordwood Forest. Near the next station, on an eminence beside the river, stands up the ancient fane of Newchurch, a parish that, in spite of its name, is old enough to have once included both Ryde and Ventnor in its ample bounds. Then by Harringford Station below Arreton Down,

The East Side

the line comes to Merston Junction, there forking north and south.

In old days Sandown, then known rather as Sandham, was distinguished by a "castle," which has given place to less imposing but more formidable modern forts, serving as models for sand-engineering to the troops of children encamped here in summer. Its only other historical association seems to be as retreat of the notorious John Wilkes in his old age, cheered by more gentle pursuits than might be expected of a so unedifying demagogue. He was given to rearing pigeons, as well as to collecting books and china, at his Sandown "Villakin," a sort of tawdry miniature of Horace Walpole's show, to which the owner's notoriety attracted many visitors. One describes him as walking about his grounds "in Arcadian costume," raking up weeds with a hoe and destroying vipers. He complained that the pigeons he got from England, Ireland, and France always took the first chance of flying home, so that he had almost given up pigeon-keeping, "when I bethought myself to procure a cock and hen pouter from Scotland : I need not add that *they never returned.*" This cockney bitterness against North Britons, it will be remembered, made a common subject between Dr Johnson and the ex-Lord Mayor, when Boswell had his wish of bringing them together. Wilkes showed one visitor a pond in the garden stocked with carp, tench, perch, and eels, because, he said, fish could not be had by the seaside. Here he also employed himself in writing the memoirs which he had the decency to destroy. The toothless old rip, with one foot in the grave, bragged how his squinting eye had done great execution with the pretty farmers' daughters at Newport market: well known is his boast, that, monster of ugliness as he was, he could "talk away his face," so as to be only a quarter of an hour behind the handsomest man. Another story is that when, on his last crossing of the Solent, the vessel was becalmed, he jocularly affected to take this as a presage of death, since he had never been able to live in a calm; but his retreat at Sandown seems to have been quiet enough for Cowper or Hannah More.

If, to set off against that ribald sojourner of its neighbour's, Shanklin wanted to boast a notorious character, it was a generation ago the headquarters, as perhaps rather it would prefer to forget, of one of the most audacious criminals of our time, whose life, so far as I know, has never been written, unless in criminal calendars. His real name, it appears, was Benson, which does not figure in the Dictionary of National Biography, though it deserves a place there beside Claude Duval's and George Barrington's; while I am mistaken if it were not qualified by nationality. On this side of the Channel he called himself a Frenchman; but he spoke French and English equally well, as would hardly have been the case, had he not passed his youth in England. He was certainly a Jew, of typically Jewish aspect. His adventurous career would make a theme for the pen that chronicled Jonathan Wild's; and if I offer a sketch of it, *faute de mieux*, it is because I had the advantage of knowing him. He did me the honour of trying to make me one of his dupes, in which enterprise, I am glad to say, he succeeded less well than in other cases; and I did not care to cultivate an acquaintance which he pressed upon me. But with a little help from hearsay and surmise, I believe I can supply an outline of his history, wrapped as it was in clouds of deceit.

He was, I am told, the son of a prosperous Jewish tradesman established at Paris, who had means to put him in a position of respectability, if not of wealth, "instead of which," young Benson from his youth took to knavery like a duck to the water. I have heard that in early life he had been connected with the French or the Belgian press; and he showed some familiarity with journalism, which he sought to turn to account in his swindling schemes. That part of his life, indeed, lies in deep shadow, which might be cleared up by research among police *dossiers* of the continent.

His first notable *coup* in England seems to have been during the Franco-Prussian War, when he flew at such high game as the very Lord Mayor. A French town had been burned by the Prussians. While this disaster was still fresh on our news sheets, there burst into the Mansion House a voluble gentleman professing to be the mayor of that town, come to throw himself on the generosity of the great English nation. Our sympathetic Lord Mayor handed out a thousand pounds; and it was whispered at the time that this plausible guest carried off also the heart of his lordship's daughter. The clever trick ended in detection, arrest, and two years' imprisonment; then by way of varying the monotony of Newgate, Benson tried to set fire to his cell, but succeeded only in burning himself about the spine, so as to be henceforth a helpless cripple. There were some who surmised that he made the most of this injury as helping out his disguise of deceit; but I never saw his slight figure unless as recumbent on a couch, or carried like a child in the arms of a big Frenchman, who passed as his valet, being really one of the swindling gang of which Benson was the brain. His crippled state was put down to a railway accident.

After his release from Newgate comes a period of obscurity, from which he emerges about 1875 as living in some style at Shanklin, with a London *pied à terre* in Cavendish Square, a brougham, and everything genteel about him. It was at this time I made his acquaintance. He then passed under the name of Yonge, with some explanation which I forget; but he confided to me and to others how he was really the Count de Montague, a Frenchman engaged in conspiring for the Empire, business that was to account for the seclusion in which he lived. This struck me as dubious: in those days, before dynamite outrages, one could conspire at the pitch of one's voice in the middle of Piccadilly without anyone caring to interfere. Moreover, in writing to me, he signed himself *De Montagu*, whereas, for a more favoured friend, he decorated the name with a final *e.* It took little Sherlock Holmes' faculty to detect that a French nobleman ought to know how to spell his own name; but I am glad to say that from my first sight of the "Count," I distrusted a gentleman whose dress and manners seemed too fine to be true. He never deceived me by his pretensions; and his overdone elegance served to set others on their guard. Indeed, like Joseph Andrews, he might have passed for a nobleman with one who had not seen many noblemen.

For not being taken in by him, I have perhaps to thank my deficiencies. His chief accomplishment, it seems, was playing the piano like an angel, which left me cold, while it drew tuneful flies into his web of treasons and stratagems. Some women were much taken by his feline manners, which on others produced such a feeling of repulsion as was my experience. One family became so captivated as to act as his social sponsors in the Isle of Wight, where he was received with open arms. If I remember right, it was a house belonging to this family which he tenanted; and rumour went that his admiring landlady's eyes were hardly opened even by the exposure that cost her dear. Several writers for the press were brought into relations with him through a well-known author, who has to confess that he allowed his honesty to be deceived. When urged to search closer into Benson's antecedents, he was content to let himself be put off with audacity. "Go to the French Ambassador!" exclaimed that plausible knave; but no such inquiry was carried out; and his most solid credentials were from a London bank, that knew nothing of him but his having a considerable balance to draw upon.

How he got the means to figure thus as a wealthy foreigner, I know not; but I have a good guess as to a main aim of his schemes which never came to light. At this time he was concerned in founding a periodical which was to champion religion, loyalty, honesty, and other causes he professed to have at heart. He knew very little about the higher walks of the press; and his design wavered between a newspaper and a half-crown monthly. In the latter form the organ financed by him did appear, soon to be eclipsed. Its name and short history are best forgotten. The pious founder, not being so ready with his pen as with his tongue, proposed to me to write an article on certain money-market matters, the tone and facts of which article were to be dictated by him. He was such a shallow knave that he did not take the precaution of carefully testing my likelihood to be a fit tool in his hands; and at my first interview with him, he took for granted that I knew nothing of French; then, by the way in which he and his valet *parlez-voused* to each other before my face, I soon got a suspicion they were not master and servant.

By no means prepossessed in his favour by the ease with which he reckoned on catching me, I refused to enlist myself as literary bravo in affairs quite beyond my scope. He did find a more subservient scribe to write such an article as he had outlined, which the publisher refused to print as libellous; then Benson was for bringing an action against the firm by way of advertisement for his organ, now launched with a great flourish of trumpets. This was at a time when certain papers had done more or less good service, to themselves and the public, by exposing scandals in the financial world. On that example, I believe Benson aimed at gaining a character for audacious honesty, then using it to rig the money-market to his own profit *quo cumque modo*, or to levy blackmail in a manner since perfected by certain "financial" papers that are the disgrace of our journalism.

I never understood why he took some pains to enlist me as his accomplice, or could imagine that he had found in me a congenial spirit. More than once he asked me to his house in the Isle of Wight; but it proved well that I never accepted any hospitality from him. To oblige my friend the editor, whose only fault in the matter was a generous trustfulness, I did write for his organ on subjects in my own line; but my misgivings held me back from personal intercourse with the proprietor. The last time I saw him was at a dinner party, some way out of London, given to make him acquainted with the staff of his literary enterprise. He had now come to whispering that he was no less than a prince, who for certain reasons preferred to be *incognito;* and some of us needy scribblers were much impressed by his condescension. He pressed on me the honour of having a lift back to town in his carriage, which I accepted very unwillingly, so strong had grown my suspicions. On our drive, I remember, the main drift of his conversation was contempt for the company we had just left; and he abused the host for asking the like of him to meet such outsiders; but I did not respond to the flattery implied in such confidences, with which once more he seemed inviting me to intimacy. I congratulated myself on my reserve, when next week a reward of £1000 was offered for the arrest of this pseudo-prince, set in his true light by a notorious trial that followed in the spring of 1877, after he had been run to earth in Scotland, somewhere about the Bridge of Allan.

This was known as the Turf Frauds case; but I forgot the precise details of the ingenious swindle which Benson, along with several accomplices, was convicted of practising on a French lady, the Comtesse de Goncourt. As ringleader, and as formerly convicted of forgery, he was sentenced to fifteen years' imprisonment. In the course of the trial, it came out that he had managed to corrupt some of the minor officials of Newgate, and to keep up relations outside, by whose help this cripple had plotted a daring escape. Then, his fate being decided, he sought to gain some remission of his punishment by turning informer on another set of accomplices; and the public was amazed, not to say dismayed, to learn that several of the detective inspectors of Scotland Yard had been in this scoundrel's pay, hobnobbing with him as his guests, and serving warnings on him instead of the warrants entrusted to them. The story is too long to tell that came out in a three weeks' sensational trial at the end of the same year. One or two of the accused detectives got off in a cloud of suspicion; but the others, as well as a solicitor who had been leagued with them, convicted chiefly on Benson's evidence, were sentenced to two years' imprisonment, from which a couple of ex-inspectors emerged to start in the shady profession of private inquiry agents.

I am not sure if Benson served his full term in England; but it was many years afterwards that I heard of him as having again got into trouble in Switzerland. This time, he must have come off easily, for when three or four more years had passed, he is seen seeking fortune in the New World. Here his last trick was as ingenious and bold as his first appearance at the Mansion House. A great singer, Madame Patti if I mistake not, was eagerly expected at the Opera House of Mexico City. A few days in advance of her, came to the Iturbide Hotel a polite gentleman giving himself out as her agent. This was Benson, who, having sold all the boxes and stalls, made off with his plunder in a special train, and managed to get out of the country, but was arrested, I understand, in New York, to be held for extradition. It is probable that Mexican penal servitude has terrors even for habitués of Newgate and Dartmoor. At all events, poor Benson, in despair, committed suicide by throwing himself over a landing in his prison. So ended my would-be host in the Isle of Wight, where he entertained worthier guests than me, not to speak of his train of friendly detectives.

This is but an ugly story to tell of such a pretty place as Shanklin, an older and a choicer resort than Sandown, favoured by visitors both in winter and summer, and with a good share of permanent residents attracted by its charms. As in the case of Lynton and Lynmouth, Shanklin has a double character. By the sea has sprung up a new bathing-place with a smart esplanade, showy pier, a disfiguringly convenient lift to the top of the cliff, and everything spick and span. The old Shanklin behind offers a contrast in its nucleus of embowered cottages, and its irregular High Street hugging an inland hollow, about which villas are half-buried in blooming gardens and clumps of foliage, like the huge myrtles that enclose the little parsonage near the churchyard in its grove of gravestones. But for some rawer rows of houses stretching out towards the cliff, upper Shanklin has lost little of the charm that struck Lord Jeffrey,

SHANKLIN VILLAGE—MOONLIGHT
AFTER RAIN

when he described the village as "very small and *scattery*, all mixed up with trees, and lying among sweet airy falls and swells of ground which finally rise up behind the breezy Downs 800 feet high, and sink down in front to the edge of the varying cliffs which overhang a pretty beach of fine sand, and are approachable by a very striking wooded ravine which they call the Chine."

An earlier visitor was Keats, who is understood to have written his *Lamia* in a cottage, not now standing, about the opening rechristened "Keats' Green" in honour of this sojourn, when, to tell the truth, he wrote of the Isle of Wight as "but so, so," though he admired the coast from Shanklin to Bonchurch, as well he might. Longfellow, who wrote an inscription for a fountain near his hotel, called Shanklin "one of the quietest and loveliest places in the kingdom," with which, indeed, his acquaintance had not been exhaustive.

Shanklin and Sandown, the most growing resorts of the Island of late years, love one another like Liverpool and Manchester, like Ramsgate and Margate, like St Paul's and Minneapolis, and other pairs of too near rivals for popularity. Careful parents may prefer Sandown as a place where their youngsters will find nothing to fall off; but poetic and artistic souls will give their vote for Shanklin, which has chalybeate springs and elaborate baths as attraction, as well as beautiful surroundings. Its beauty spot *par excellence* is, of course, the Chine above mentioned, which makes one of the shows of the Island. The Chines, so named here and on the opposite mainland coast—but in one part of Hampshire *Bunny* is a less romantic title for them—are deep, irregular ravines carved out by streams of water upon cliffs of soft clay or sand, often sheltering a profusion of tangled vegetation, or again, as at Bournemouth, revealing the frame of naked nature. The Shanklin Chine, in the former variety, is by many judged the prettiest, as it is perhaps the best known to visitors. A description of it may be borrowed from Black's *Guide to the Isle of Wight*.

This popular sight, like other wonders of nature on the Island, is enclosed, a small charge being made for admission, and in more than one respect rather suggests the tea-garden order of resort, but nothing can spoil it. It is to be entered at either end, but excursion coaches usually bring their passengers to the head of the Chine. At the top will be found a ferruginous spring. Here the chasm is at its narrowest, increasing till it has a breadth of nearly 300 feet, while the steep sides are in parts almost 200 feet high. Winding walks take one for some quarter of a mile down a deep glen, which differs notably from Blackgang Chine in being choked up with trees and a rich undergrowth of ferns, moss, and brushwood, wherever any shade-loving plant can take root. Into the top pours a little waterfall, rushing to the sea at the bottom of this wilderness of greenery.

But even without its Chine, Shanklin would have a right to be proud of itself. It lies at the corner of the southern range of Downs that separate it from Ventnor and the Undercliff. Open and airy walks may be taken on these heights; or less arduous strolls by the leafy knolls and hollows on their flanks. One favourite ramble is to Cook's Castle, an artificial ruin

SHANKLIN CHINE

upon a wooded brow commanding a fine view, whence it is a short mile to Wroxall, the next station on the railway as it bends inland, to find nothing for it but a tunnel through the heights that shelter Ventnor.

From the bottom of Shanklin Chine, when the tide is out, one can follow the coast round the fissured crags of Dunnose, on which a cliff-walk is always open. Thus is reached Luccombe Chine, a modestly retiring scene, not so easily found, since there is no charge for admission; but well worth finding. Beyond this one enters the tangled wilderness of the Landslip, through which winds a path for Bonchurch. But here we come within the purlieus of Ventnor, and round to the "Back of the Island."

From the heights at this corner, one looks down upon the scene of one of the saddest of naval disasters in our day, recorded in churchyards that show the tombs of so many young lives. Off Dunnose was lost, in 1878, the training ship *Eurydice*, with her company of hearty and hopeful lads. I well remember how that Sunday afternoon the March wind blustered on the northern heights of London. But under the lee of the Undercliff, the homeward bound sailors hailed it as a favouring breeze; then with ports open and under all plain canvas, the *Eurydice* spanked on round Dunnose, passing out of shelter of the Downs, to be taken aback by a snow squall, that threw her on her beam-ends before the men could shorten sail. Many of them must have been drowned as they rushed to struggle up on deck, from which others were swept away, blinded by the snow, or drawn down in the vortex of the sinking vessel. Three or four came to be picked up, an hour later, by a passing collier, and only two lived to tell the amazement of their sudden wreck, whose victims had much the same fate as those of the *Royal George.*

Gone in a moment ! hurried headlong down
From light and hope to darkness and despair !
Plunged into utter night without renown,
Bereft of all—home, country, earth, and air—
Without a warning, yea, without a prayer !

THE UNDERCLIFF

THE "Back of the Island" is a familiar name given locally to the south coast, its eastern end more widely famed as the Undercliff. All this side is marked by sterner features and sharper outlines than the shallow creeks and flats of the northern shore; and through its geological history the Undercliff makes a peculiar exhibition of picturesqueness, while by its winter climate it is one of England's most favoured nooks.

Here a narrow strip of shore lies for miles walled in to the north by a steep bank several hundred feet high, sometimes presenting a rugged face of sandstone cliff, elsewhere rising in the turf swell of chalk downs. But the bastions of rock thus displayed rest upon a treacherous foundation of gault clay, expressively known as the "Blue slipper," which, saturated with water, has given way so as to cause repeated landslides and falls of the superincumbent strata, tumbling the lower slopes into a broken chaos of terraces and knolls, dotted with boulders of chalk and sandstone. This ruin of nature has long been overgrown by rich greenery, mantling its asperities, all the more since the charms and mildness of the situation go to making it a much trimmed wilderness, populated with villages and villas that turn the Undercliff into one great garden of choice and luxuriant vegetation.

The capital of the Undercliff is Ventnor, whose dependencies and outposts straggle almost all along this sheltered coast-strip. Now the most beautifully placed and the most widely admired town in the Island, it has risen to such note within the memory of men still living. A century ago Sir H. Englefield gives it a word as "a neat hamlet," while guidebooks of his day do not even name it between the older villages of St Lawrence and Bonchurch, that on either side wing its body of terraces and zigzag streets. Its history seems illustrated in the old "Crab and Lobster" Inn, from a modest haunt of fishermen developed into a spacious hotel, and still more plainly in the monuments of so many a young life close packed about its nineteenth century churches. It was Sir James Clarke, an esteemed physician of our great-grandfathers' day, who dubbed Ventnor an English Madeira, and brought it into medical repute as a rival of Torquay, both of them disputing the honour of having the mildest winter climate in England, which probably belongs rather to the Cornish coast, or to other claimants still wanting a *vates sacer*, that is, a London doctor to give them bold advertisement.

The shift in medical opinion as to the cure of

The Undercliff

consumption by pure and dry air, however cold, must have somewhat blown upon Ventnor's reputation; and it may in future come to depend upon its amenities as much as on the soft climate, now that Mentone itself seems rather shy of its old character as a rendezvous for consumptive germs. It has a summer as well as a winter season; but there is not much to be said for its bathing and boating, the shore here being rougher than on the east side, and exposed to dangerous currents. The beach before the esplanade has been tamed a little and brought under the yoke of bathing machines. Further along there are here and there tempting strips of sand; but swimmers may be cautioned as to launching forth too trustfully. The same hint applies to boating, this coast being best navigated with the help of someone who knows its reefs and eddies. Ventnor visitors are more ready to make jaunts on land than by sea; and in fine weather their favourite amusement is supplied by the coaches, brakes, and other vehicles which carry them to all parts of the Island. There are daily excursions in the season to Freshwater, Cowes, and other remote points; besides morning and afternoon trips to Blackgang, Shanklin, and such nearer goals; and the stranger will have much ado to deny the insinuating recruiters who at every corner of the High Street lie in wait to enlist him for their crew of pleasure-seekers.

The strong point of the town is its picturesque site, which, indeed, implies the defects of its qualities,

having been termed "fit for kangaroos" by some
short-winded critic. Nature never meant herself
here to be laid out in streets, and eligible plots of
building land have to be taken as they can be found
on the steep slope. This fact, however favourable
to scenic effect, proves a little trying to those feeble
folk who make so large a part of the population.
Communication with the different levels of the town,
where the climate varies according to their degree
of elevation and protection, has to be effected by
steep stairs, winding ascents, and devious roads;
and often one's goal seems provokingly near, while
it turns out to be tiresomely far by the only available
access. One thoroughfare is so precipitous that a
railing has been provided for the aid of those risking
its descent. The twisting High Street debouches
into a hollow, prettily laid out, about which are the
most sheltered parts of the town. Here stands the
pier with its shelters and pavilion; and a short
esplanade curves round the little bay to a rocky
point, from which other zigzags remount to the
higher quarters. There has been a proposal to
extend this esplanade along the Bonchurch side of
the shore, where the gasworks certainly do not form
a very pleasant or convenient obstruction; but on
the whole it appears better to leave Ventnor as it
is. Its great charm consists of being as unlike as
possible to the general type of seaside resorts; and
its irregular architecture, wilful roads, and provoking
impasses are at least in harmony with each other.

The Undercliff

Let us see how it strikes a stranger—Mr W. D. Howells, to wit—on a recent visit.

The lovely little town, which is like an English water-colour, for the rich, soft blur of its greys and blues and greens, has a sea at its feet of an almost Bermudian variety of rainbow tints, and a milky horizon all its own, with the sails of fishing-boats drowning in it like moths that had got into the milk. The streets rise in amphitheatrical terraces from the shore, and where they cease to have the liveliness of watering-place shops, they have the domesticity of residential hotels and summer boarding-houses, and private villas set in depths of myrtle and holly and oleander and laurel: some of the better-looking houses were thatched, perhaps to satisfy a sentiment for rusticity in the summer boarder or tenant.

But this appreciative stranger is a little at sea in freely dashing into his sketch a background of "seats and parks of nobility and gentry," which seems somewhat of an American exaggeration for the villaed skirts of Ventnor. The most lordly "seat" about Ventnor is Steephill Castle, at the west end, from the tower of which flaunts his own Stars and Stripes to proclaim it the home of a compatriot who must have reason to chuckle, as he does in a volume of memoirs, that slow, simple, honest John Bull now wakes up to let himself be exploited by Transatlantic enterprise. This gentleman's daughter was the late popular novelist "John Oliver Hobbes," who latterly lived much here, or in the neighbourhood. The modern castle, that has housed an empress in its time, took the place of a cottage of gentility built by Hans Stanley, George III.'s Governor of the Island. It formerly belonged to the Hamborough family, whose heir met with his

F

death in a painful way, that gave rise to what was known as the Ardlamont murder case.

The trustees of this family have lately been at loggerheads with the Ventnor people as to enclosing the links by the shore. Part of the cliff here, however, has been acquired as a prettily unconventional public park, laid out with playing greens beneath its leafy mazes and airy walks. At this end, opposite the west gate of the park, is the station of the mid-island line, distinguished as "Ventnor Town," whereas "Ventnor" station of the older east coast rail stands so high above the sea that access to it suggests the "stations" of a pilgrimage. The last time I was in Ventnor, I had the pleasure of being able to assist some countrywomen of Mr Howell's whom I found fluttering in breathless doubt between those two confusing goals, that ought to be joined by some kind of mountain railway.

One advantage of having attained the upper station, is that here one is half-way up the steep bank rising behind Ventnor to be the highest point of the Island, nearly 800 feet. This down bears the name of St Boniface, in honour of whom passing ships used to lower their topsails. The ridge is reached by chalky paths from a road near the station, and from other approaches at the top of the town ; and however stuffy the air may be below, the perspiring climber will not fail to find invigoration on the open crest. For goal of the ascent, there is a wishing-well, as to which old tradition has it that, if you reach

The Undercliff

the spot, Orpheus-like, without casting a backward glance, the wish you may form while drinking of its welcome spring will speedily be fulfilled. Certainly no finer view could be wished for than one gains from the summit and along a wide stretch of rambles on either hand. Holding on round a horse-shoe hollow, one may turn down on the right to Shanklin; or, in the other direction, crossing the rail and road to Ryde at Wroxall, pass over to the heights of Appuldurcombe, where the Worsley monument makes a beacon. Hence another lofty sweep brings one back to Ventnor by Week Down and Rew Down, used as a golf ground, which must try the strength of elderly devotees on their preliminary ascent to the clubhouse, standing out like an Alpine chapel.

The stiff-kneed pilgrim who has not heart for such arduosities, may follow the road along the face of St Boniface Down, or the sea-walk below, to Bonchurch, that choice and lovely east-end of Ventnor, clustered round a pond, overhung by a rich bank of foliage. The mildness of the climate is attested by huge arbutus growths, recalling those of Killarney, by fuchsias like trees, with trunks as thick as a strong man's wrist, and by scarlet geraniums of such exuberance that a single plant will cover several square yards of wall in front of a house. This one fact, more than any word-painting, gives an idea of the way in which Bonchurch, and indeed most parts of Ventnor, are embowered by foliage. In all sorts of odd nooks, either nestling against the steep wall of the Undercliff, or hiding away in its leafy hollows, perch the picturesque cottages and handsome villas that have attracted only too many neighbours. The road is much shut in between walls of private grounds, within which are enclosed some of the finest spots, such as the "Pulpit Rock," a projecting mass of sandstone marked by a cross, and another known as the " Flagstaff Rock.

Threading our way between these forbidden paradises, the road would take us up by the new Church with its sadly beautiful graveyard. A lane turns steeply downwards past the old church, now disused, one of the many smallest churches in England, that has the further note of being the sole wholly Norman structure in the Island. Here are buried the Rev. W. Adams, author of the *Shadow of the Cross*, and John Sterling, Carlyle's friend, who came to die at Hillside, now a boarding-house near the upper station at Ventnor. Another literary celebrity who lived here was Elizabeth Sewell, whose *Amy Herbert* and other edifying novels were so popular in her own generation ; and in one of them, *Ursula*, she has described the scenery about her home.

The old church is said to be now in danger of slipping down towards the sea. Below it, one descends to Monks' Bay, traditional landing-place of the French Benedictines who made themselves once so much at home on the Island, as their spiritual descendants are doing now. The sea-walk round

BONCHURCH OLD CHURCH
NEAR VENTNOR

this bay leads into the Landslip, so called *par excellence*, as the rawest and wildest disturbance of the Undercliff, its last fall being not yet a century old. This wilderness of overgrown knolls and hillocks, tumbled from the crags above, is not to be equalled on our south coast unless by the similar chaos near Lyme Regis, whose broken and bosky charms have been stirred into fresh picturesqueness by slips of more recent date. Over daisied turf one here takes a twisting path that leads by banks of bracken and bramble into thickets of gnarled thorn and other blossoming shade, half-burying green mounds and grey boulders in a tangle where one would soon lose oneself but for occasional glimpses of the sea below, or for running upon the wall of a private enclosure behind, guide for the wanderer in his descent towards Luccombe Chine, who can also ascend to the cliff-walk for Shanklin. The scene is thus described by Thomas Webster, a geologist who visited it a century ago, while the first convulsion was still fresh, before the last slip of 1818 came to make confusion worse confounded.

A considerable portion of the cliff had fallen down, strewing the whole of the ground between it and the sea with its ruins ; huge masses of solid rock started up amidst heaps of smaller fragments ; whilst immense quantities of loose marl, mixed with stones, and even the soil above with the wheat still growing on it, filled up the spaces between, and formed hills of rubbish which are scarcely accessible. Nothing had resisted the force of the falling rocks. Trees were levelled with the ground, and many lay half buried in the ruins. The streams were choked up, and pools of water were formed in many places. Whatever road or path formerly existed through this place had been effaced ; and with some difficulty I passed over this avalanche, which extended many hundred yards. Proceeding east-wards, the whole of the soil seemed to have been moved, and was filled with chasms and bushes lying in every direction. The intricate and rugged path became gradually less distinct, and soon divided into mere sheep tracks, leading into an almost impenetrable thicket. I perceived, however, on my left hand, the lofty wall of rock which belonged to the same stratum as the Undercliff, softened in its rugged character by the foliage which grew in its fissures, and still preserving some remains of its former picturesque beauty. Neglect, and the unfortunate accident which had lately happened, had now altered the features of this once delightful spot ; and I was soon bewildered among rocks, streams of water, tangling thorns, and briars.

The labyrinth between Luccombe and Bonchurch was not the only landslip in modern times ; and though there is believed to be little fear of any further serious disturbance, occasional falls of rock are a warning how this gracious ruin of nature might be renewed. *The* Landslip here[1] makes to my mind the *bouquet* of the whole Undercliff, whose similar features, on an ampler scale, of older wrinkles, and usually more veiled by the work of man, stretch for miles westward along a rugged platform varying up to half a mile in width. Words but feebly paint the charms of a miniature Riviera, its broken land-waves foaming into groves, gardens, and tangles of shrubbery. Between the wall of downs and cliff-buttresses shutting it in to the north, and the sea dashing at its foot, the foliage runs as rank as in a giant's greenhouse, beautifully

[1] There is a model of this broken corner of the shore on the ground floor of the Geological Museum in Jermyn Street, but hardly on a large enough scale to display its beauty.

THE LANDSLIP NEAR VENTNOR

The Undercliff

displayed by the accidents of the irregularly sloping ground.

> Crags, knolls, and mounds confusedly hurl'd,
> The fragments of an earlier world.

This line of cliffs may indeed remind us of the Trossachs, with one side opened out to the sun and a richer vegetation at its base. Hawthorns, elders, and other bushes grow here to a huge height, dappling the green of the woods with their blossoms. Myrtle and other semi-tropical plants flourish hardily; everywhere there are flowers prodigal as weeds, notably the red Valerian flourishing on walls and broken edges. Huge boulders are half hidden in ivy, heaps of old ruins are buried in almost impassable thickets. It is hard to say when the huge bank of greenery is most beautiful—whether in spring with all its blossoms and tender buds; or in summer wearing its full glory of leafage; or again in autumn brilliant with changing tints and spangled by bright berries: even in winter there are evergreens enough to make us forget the cold winds banished from this cosy nook. The one blot on such a paradise seems the many notices to trespassers, warning that its most tempting nooks are "private," or the still more ominous placards of "valuable building land to let on lease."

The Bonchurch Landslip must be traversed on foot. On the other side of Ventnor, a good road winds up and down beneath the inland heights, from the edge of which one better sees how many houses and gardens are hidden away here in their own greenery. Other aspects are presented from a path rising and falling along the broken cliffs of the shore. The road, in fine weather, will be astir with coaches, brakes, and other wheels making for Blackgang Chine, that renowned goal of excursions from all over the Island. Beyond Steephill Castle, it leads through St Lawrence, the western, as Bonchurch is the eastern wing of Ventnor.

St Lawrence, known to guide-books that used to pass Ventnor Cove without a word, has another of the smallest churches in England, now replaced by a new one. The old church, till slightly enlarged by Lord Yarborough, measured twenty feet by twelve under a roof which must have obliged a tall knight to doff his helmet. Its saint, like St Boniface, gave his name to a well now enclosed under a Gothic arch. But the great institution of the parish, standing in a long terrace by the roadside, is the Hospital for Consumption, which Ventnor people insist on as being at St Lawrence, just as Woking pushes off the honour of the Brookwood Cemetery. There was a time when this model hospital made an advertisement for Ventnor; now new notions as to germ-infection tend to scare away more profitable guests than its patients, who might be expected to fall off under new theories of treatment for consumption, but the building has had a recent addition in memory of Prince Henry of Battenberg.

We are now among mansions and cottages of

The Undercliff

thick-set gentility, the nucleus of which was a villa built by Sir R. Worsley, who made the hardly successful experiment of planting a vineyard here. The oldest structure seems to be a little ivy-clad ruin at Woolverton on the shore, as to the character of which antiquaries for once have differed like doctors, while its antiquity, like that of the old church, offers hopeful promise for the permanence of modern buildings on these oft-torn slopes. But we must not stop to speak of every house on this road, nor of every private pleasance like that known to Swinburne—

> The shadowed lawns, the shadowing pines, the ways
> That wind and wander through a world of flowers,
> The radiant orchard where the glad sun's gaze
> Dwells, and makes most of all his happiest hours ;
> The field that laughs beneath the cliff that towers,
> The splendour of the slumber that enthralls
> With sunbright peace the world within their walls,
> Are symbols yet of years that love recalls.

On one hand, ascents like the "Cripple Path" would lead us to fine prospects from the cliff-brow, while below, we might seek out Puckaster Cove, or the Buddle Inn near a good stretch of sand, such as is rather exceptional hereabouts, where fragments of the destruction above are found trailing out into the sea to form dangerous reefs. One theory makes Puckaster the Roman tin-shipping port ; and it certainly proved a haven of refuge for Charles II. in a storm, as recorded in a neighbouring parish-register. Along the broken slope, the high-road takes us as described by William Black, who has caught the characteristic features of so many English scenes.

There was a great quiet prevailing along these southern shores. They drove by underneath the tall and crumbling precipices, with wood-pigeons suddenly shooting out from the clefts, and jackdaws wheeling about far up in the blue. They passed by sheltered woods, bestarred with anemones and primroses, and showing here and there the purple of the as yet half-opened hyacinth ; they passed by lush meadows, all ablaze with the golden yellow of the celandine and the purple of the ground-ivy ; they passed by the broken, picturesque banks where the tender blue of the speedwell was visible from time to time, with the white glimmer of the star-wort. And then all this time they had on their left a gleaming and wind-driven sea, full of motion, and light, and colour, and showing the hurrying shadows of the flying clouds.

The goal of Black's party was the Sandrock Hotel, prettily situated by the roadside at Undercliff Niton, which has a chalybeate spring, and near it some local worthy thought desirable to erect a small shrine to the memory of Shakespeare, anticipating the more pretentious monument by which he is now to be glorified in London. From this seaside outpost turns off the way to the inland village of Niton, lying behind in a break of the chalk heights. It has been distinguished from Knighton by the sobriquet of Crab Niton, "a distinction which the inhabitants do not much relish, and therefore it will be impolitic to employ it," as a venerable guide-book very prudently suggests ; and Knighton being nowadays little more than a name, strangers will find no inconvenience in taking that hint. The place boasts at least one sojourner of note, as we learn from the

THE UNDERCLIFF NEAR VENTNOR

tomb of Edward Edwards, leader of the Free Public Library movement that has now so many monuments all over the country.

The parish of Niton is a large one, containing the head springs of the Medina and of the eastern Yar, which the well-greaved adventurer might hence try to track across the Island to their not very distant mouths. More otiose travellers will find a road passing under St Catherine's Down for Newport and the central parts. From the sturdy church tower with its low spire, a lane leads up to the top of the Down, whence we could take a wide view of our wanderings, backwards and forwards. And here, since we are almost at the end of the Undercliff, let us break off to survey the longer but less famed stretch of this coast, westwards, under its more comprehensive title.

THE BACK OF THE ISLAND

OUR Pisgah for this stage is St Catherine's Down, once held the highest point of the Island, but now dethroned, like Ben Macdhui, in favour of the Ben Nevis of St Boniface. It appears that in Georgian days Week Down was charged with hiding Shanklin Down from the view of St Catherine's, as is no longer the case, the moral being that one or other of these heights has been raised or depressed, as may well have happened to superstructures upon so slippery foundation. In such a question of measurements, at all events, "the self-styled science of the so-called nineteenth century" with its more elaborate observations, gives a surer title to eminence. But St Catherine's is only a few feet lower than the ridge above Ventnor ; and from it, too, a fine prospect may be had, ranging over the Isle of Wight to the heights of the mainland, and across the Channel to the French coast in clear weather.

This broad and steep block of down is well provided with landmarks. On the inland side a tall pillar was erected by a Russian merchant, in honour of the Czar Alexander's visit to England after the

The Back of the Island

fall of Napoleon; which monument a later generation very inappropriately adorned with a memorial of our soldiers fallen in the Crimean War. On the top are the restored remains of a chapel, where in old days a hermit-priest made himself truly useful by keeping a light burning to warn mariners off this stormy coast, and chanting prayers for their safety. A less pious legend attributes the building of the old beacon here to a layman amerced in such a penalty for having stored his cellars with wine sold him by shipwrecked sailors, a class not very scrupulous as to owner's rights—

> Full many a draught of wine had he y-draw
> From Bourdeaux-ward, while that the chapmen sleep :
> Of nicé conscience took he no keep.

Hard by is a later ruin to show how a lighthouse was designed in the eighteenth century, but a practical age gave up the attempt to rear a pharos on this cloudy height. Experience since then has gone to show that a lighthouse serves its end better at the water's edge than on commanding cliffs like Beachy Head and Portland Point, from both of which the old beacons have lately been moved to a lower level.

St Catherine's Lighthouse stands on the point of that ilk, the most southerly projection of the Island, where it has Lloyd's signal station for neighbour. Its recently intensified electric light is said to be the most powerful in the world, every few seconds flashing over the sea a beam of concentrated glare equal to millions of candles. It is also equipped with a fog-horn, whose hoarse note of warning resounds for miles, not altogether to the satisfaction of neighbours safe on land. Yet they may take comfort to think how this screech is more fearsomely disquieting when heard at sea. I once had such a note ringing in my ears for two days together running through a chill fog off Newfoundland, with icebergs about us that could be felt but not seen. Our boat was one of the few that have crushed into an iceberg and crawled to land with the tale; then to keep us cheerful we had on board a survivor of that adventure, the perils whereof it pleased him to depict as looming through a somewhat befogged imagination.

Another of our fellow-passengers was an American gentleman, who in Europe had been qualifying himself to come out as an opera tenor. He was coy of giving us a specimen of his talent, till one night we persuaded him to begin *Ah, che la morte!* But at once the officer of the watch stepped up to silence him, explaining that his singing might drown the sound of fog-horns. The vocalist was much offended at his organ being coupled with a fog-horn; and I fear I gave him fresh offence by suggesting "Signor Fogorno" as a suitable *nom de guerre*, when he consulted me as to Italianising his rather commonplace patronymic. But that careful officer was right, if the story be true that a German liner ran ashore on the back of the Island because her own brass band deafened her to the warning note that surely should have drowned all sweeter sounds. And if our insulted tenor had known it, this artificial organ has a very old theatrical connection, for *persona* seems the earliest form of such a sounding contrivance, originally a megaphonic mouthpiece fitted to a mask which, as one of the classical stage properties, came to denote the personage thus represented; and in time the name gained respectability as the person or parson of a parish, who more or less loudly warned his convoy of souls from the rocks and shoals of ill-doing.

A different kind of signal would be keenly watched for in days when the storm of Napoleon's invasion was expected to burst upon our shores; and on all prominent points beacons were kept ready to spread the alarm of the enemy's approach. The Isle of Wight was fully on the alert, remembering how often it had been a vulnerable point in mail-clad wars with France, though one would think that the bugbear, Boney, knew his business too well to seek a difficult landing in an island, beyond which he would be brought up by a dangerous channel, a strong arsenal, and a naval rendezvous. It is said that the signalman at St Catherine's, probably having drunk the king's health too freely in smuggled spirits, mistook some fishing-boats for a French fleet, and lighted his beacon to set men mustering in arms and women and children flying for refuge to Newport. Sir Walter Scott tells us how the same sort of blunder stirred a great part

of Scotland. But on one side of the Island the scare
did not spread far, since the watcher at Freshwater
very sensibly reasoned that the wind then blowing
would keep this coast clear of hostile ships, and
forbore to pass on the alarm.

Before the building of St Catherine's lighthouse in
1840, shipwrecks were terribly common on the Island.
A famous one was that of the *Clarendon* West India-
man, in 1836. Fourteen vessels in one night are said
to have gone ashore on Chale Bay. This is no coast
for amateur mariners. One is warned also against
bathing as dangerous hereabouts, yet I, unconscious,
have swum below Blackgang in my hot youth; while
in cooler age I echo the caution. The hero of *Maud*,
whose haunts we are now approaching, would sometimes have been all the better and wiser for a morning
dip to cool his fevered brow; but he was not so much
out of conceit with life as to venture a bathe—

> Listening now to the tide in its broad-flung, shipwrecking roar,
> Now to the scream of a maddened beach dragged down by
>   the wave.

—a sound which, Tennyson states, can sometimes
be heard nine miles inland.

Chale Bay, in which is Blackgang Chine, opens on
the west side of St Catherine's Point, where, at
Rocken End, the Undercliff seems tumbling into the
sea in a chaos of blocks of chalk and sandstone
stormed upon by the waves with freshly ruinous fury.
Above, on the side of St Catherine's Down, the
scenery alters from nests of Riviera greenery to bare

BLACKGANG CHINE

The Back of the Island

slopes broken by huge boulders and scars, that expose
the geological structure of the Downs to a spectacled
eye. Here a slip of 100 acres happened at the end of
the eighteenth century; and the masterful south-west
blasts keep the ruin still somewhat raw, not skinned
over as in more sheltered nooks. The road, passing
out of shade, makes a Switzerlandish turn under the
cliffs, as it descends to Blackgang Chine, the final
goal of lion-hunters on this route.

Entrance to the so much sought sight is through
a sort of museum or bazaar, where one must either
buy something or frankly pay sixpence. This
reminds me of a visit to Pompeii more than forty
years ago—*eheu !*—when the soldier who conducted
me seemed strangely officious in repeatedly declaring
that he was not entitled to any tip; but, he added,
"I have some photographs to sell." There are those
who hint darkly at illicit entrances by which the
unprincipled or impecunious can smuggle themselves
into Blackgang Chine without paying or buying
anything; but considerate visitors will not grudge a
toll for use of the walks and steps that open up the
recesses of this great chasm, through which echoes
the boom of waves breaking on the beach below. It
differs from the Shanklin Chine in being not overgrown with greenery, but showing through its naked-
ness the various *viscera* of greenish-grey sand and
dark ferruginous clay that charm the geologist.
Description may not prove "up-to-date," as the
weather-worn sides crumble away from year to year;

yet Sir Henry Englefield's account is still to be
quoted after more than a century.

No vegetation clothes any part of this rude hollow, whose flanks
are in a state of continual decay. They are mostly composed of
very dark blue clay, through which at intervals run horizontal strata of
bright yellow sandstone, about 12 or 15 feet thick, which naturally
divide into square blocks, and have exactly the appearance of vast
courses of masonry built at different heights to sustain the
mouldering hill. What has been hitherto described may be called the
upper part of the chine, for on descending to the seashore we find
that the stratum of ironstone already mentioned, forms a cornice from
whose edge the rill falls perpendicularly 74 feet. As the sub-
stratum is of a softer material than the ironstone, being a black
indurated clay, the action of the fall has worn it into a hollow, shining
with a dusky polish from damp, and stained with the deep greens of
aquatic lichens, or the ferruginous tinge of chalybeate exudations.
The silver thread of water which falls through the air in the front of
this singular cove is, when the wind blows fresh, twisted into most
fantastic and waving curves ; and not seldom caught by the eddy and
carried up unbroken to a height greater than that from whence it fell,
and at last dissipated into mist. When a south-west wind creates a
heavy swell on the shore, the echo of the sound of the waves in this
gloomy recess is truly astonishing, and has exactly the effect of a deep
subterraneous roar issuing from the bottom of the cave. When sudden
heavy rains or the melting of snows increase the quantity of water in
the fall, the scenery of this spot must be more striking than most in
England.

Half a mile behind Blackgang Chine lies the
village of Chale, whose grey church tower stands
among the grass-grown graves of many a drowned
mariner, that seem an imitation in miniature of the
half-buried rocks and mounds of the Undercliff.
Chale is a resort on its small scale, with some good
old houses and fine scenes to attract visitors, not to
speak of a chalybeate well on the strength of which

The Back of the Island

the place once aspired to become a spa; and Dr Dabbs' opinion is emphatic that its bracing air deserves a success Chale has not yet commanded in rivalry to Shanklin or Ventnor. Its patients may at least make sure of having their fill of the south-west wind, that gives such a leeward lurch to hardier trees now that they are out of shelter in the Undercliff's sun-trap.

Westward, the shore has openings known as Walpen Chine, Ladder Chine, and Whale Chine, which are as notable as Blackgang in their way, but not so famous; and several others yawn more obscurely on the coast line to Freshwater. Some couple of miles beyond Chale, a name of grim notoriety is Atherfield Point, where many vessels have been lost on its dangerous ledge, like the German Lloyd *Eider*, in 1892, that grounded in a fog, all hands being saved, and the steamer remaining stuck fast for weeks, so as to give this neighbourhood the excitement without the horror of a great shipwreck. In bad old days the people of Chale had an evil name as wreckers, luring poor seamen to destruction by deceptive lights, and not sticking at murder as a prelude to robbery, since the law held the death of the survivors to extinguish their title in what goods might be salved.

From Chale, the seaboard opens out for a stretch of some ten miles along the Back of the Island, a part not so well known to strangers, unless as hurrying by on their way to Freshwater. But the

path along the rough shore edge is full of points of
interest, especially to the geologist, who, from
exposures of the green-sand formation passes on to
mottled earthy cliffs of the Wealden age, then again
finds sand pressed down by masses of chalk. Behind,
runs a silent military road made to link the Island
defences, which is not altogether passable for wheels ;
indeed the Freshwater end of it has tumbled into the
sea. The usual driving-road turns inland to pass
through the villages below the Downs, which now
draw back a mile or two from the beach. Let
us, then, follow Edmund Peel, the poet of this
Fair Isle.

> Back from the brink and rest the stagger'd eye
> On the green mound, whose western slope reveals
> A landscape tranquil as the deep blue sky,
> Of hill and dale a rich variety,
> Down over down, vale winding into vale,
> Where peaceful villages imbosom'd lie,
> And halls manorial, from green-swarded Chale,
> To Brixton's fruitful glebe and Brooke's delicious dale.

Behind Chale, by the outlying Chale Green near
the head of the Medina, is reached the tiny village of
Kingston with its tiny and picturesquely perched
Church, some half-dozen miles south of Newport.
The road to Freshwater turns west, soon reaching
Shorwell, in its setting of unusually rich woods, from
which rises the spire of the Church, notable for very
curious and striking features, as for its show of Leigh
monuments, a once obliterated wall-painting, and
other relics. Its vestry preserves the Gun Chamber,

SHORWELL

in which several of these Island churches once kept a cannon for defence of the coast. This village is said to have won Queen Victoria's special admiration, as well it might.

Two miles on, comes another pretty place, Brixton *alias* Brighstone, very unlike its metropolitan namesake, with a goodly Church that counts among former parsons Bishops Ken, Samuel Wilberforce, and Moberley. In the beautiful garden of the parsonage, Ken is said to have composed his far-sung Morning and Evening Hymns; and a tree is shown here under which Wilberforce wrote his *Agathos*. Hence one can descend to the shore by Grange Chine, which the military road crosses by a lofty viaduct; or over the Downs goes the road to Calbourne, the nearest station on the Freshwater line.

The next village on the road is Mottistone, from whose too much restored Church, a steep, shady lane leads up to the Mote Stone, or Long Stone, a block of ferruginous sandstone 13 feet high, with a smaller one fallen beside it, seeming to have both made part of an ancient cromlech; but this is said to have served as a mote or public meeting-place, while a natural legend sees here the stones of a diabolic and angelic putting-match on St Catherine's Down. These high downs were a favourite prehistoric burying place; and several barrows hereabouts have been excavated by a generation whose *tumuli* have shrunk to the tees of golf. The Tudor manor-house, beside Mottistone Church, is one of the best of the picturesque old structures of that period, which in this corner of the Island have not been so much shouldered off by spick-and-span villas.

Leaving the road, beyond the hamlet of Hulverston one can pass down to the shore by Brook, which has a chine to show, and a fossil forest on the west side of Brook Point, explained by the geologist Mantell as having "originated in a raft composed of a prostrate pine-forest, transported from a distance by the river which flowed through the country whence the Wealden deposits were derived, and became submerged in the sand and mud of the delta, burying with it the bones of reptiles, mussel-shells, and other extraneous bodies it had gathered in its course. . . . Many of the stems are concealed and protected by the fuci, corallines, and zoophytes which here thrive luxuriantly, and occupy the place of the lichens and other parasitical plants with which the now petrified trees were doubtlessly invested when flourishing in their native forests, and affording shelter to the Iguanodon and other gigantic reptiles." The beach yields pretty pebbles; and huge fossils have been found in the cliffs hereabouts.

Hence the military road skirts Compton Bay, upon which the Downs close in again with a steep slope of chalk that makes no safe play-place for children, especially when the turf is slippery after long drought, a caution enforced by the monument to a poor boy who fell here sixty years ago. Beyond

The Back of the Island

Afton Down, at the west end of Compton Bay, the little esplanade of Freshwater marks a new division of the Island, which, indeed, but for this much strained isthmus, would have made two islands.

FRESHWATER AND THE NEEDLES

At the south-western corner of the Island comes a cleft in the Central Downs, through which the little Yar flows across the narrowed end from Freshwater Gate, or Gap, whose name seems to denote the peculiar fact of a river having its source by the seashore, so near that in rough weather salt water is said to be washed into the stream. Through that hollow the spray of the waves can from north and south meet across the three miles of land; and unless something be done to protect such a weak spot, it appears that before long this promontory may be cut off from the Island, as itself was from the mainland by rushing Solent tides. The War Office, as one of the chief occupiers, is understood to have been more than indifferent about the sea getting its way in making the nest of forts here a miniature of the whole kingdom—

> Fortress, built by nature for herself
> Against infection or the hand of war.

In Charles I's. reign it was indeed proposed to insulate this corner artificially as a citadel of defence. Private owners and tenants, for their part, are inclined to plans for forming some kind of break-water, where the tiny esplanade of Freshwater is battered by every gale. Local authorities have been calling on the Hercules aid of a Royal Commission ; and as a beginning of defence, the Board of Trade has forbidden Freshwater Bay being used by reckless neighbours for a quarry of shingle.

Into the nook beyond, crossed each way in an hour's walk, is packed some of the finest scenery of the Island—the finest of all, some will say, who find the rich charms of the Undercliff more cloying. On the south side the Downs raise their steep wall of chalk to drop into the sea at the Needles point, round which the inner coast shows a more varied line of cliff. Between lies a huddle of very pleasant rurality, bowery lanes, hedgerow paths, thatched cottages, and thick-set hamlets, that in the very breath of the sea recall the most characteristic aspects of the green heart of England. Even the new Church has a thatched roof. But this corner, while more out of the way and the taste of trippers, is a good deal given up to Mars, whose temples here are forts and public-houses. Also it is swept by a bombardment of golf balls, which has caused punsters to suggest that this end of the Island as well as the eastern deserves the name of *Fore*land.

Freshwater itself is a modestly diffused village, which copies modern military tactics in taking very open order against the assaults of time. The main body of the place stands loosely ranked some way back from the shore, to which it throws out an advanced work held against wind and waves by hotels and a picket of bathing-machines; then a chain of rearward outposts connects it with the railway station a mile or so inland. Here the rebuilt Church, with its trappings of antiquity, makes a rallying point for hamlets in the rear, bearing such by-names as School Green, Pound Green, Sheep-wash Green and Norton, beyond which the forts on the north side, among their bivouacs of camp followers, are mixed up with lines of new building, in summer garrisoned by holiday-makers on the bathing beaches of Totland Bay and Colwell Bay.

The road from the station to the esplanade passes by a mansion hidden in "a carelessly ordered garden" among thick trees, "close to the ridge of a noble down," where

> Groves of pine on either hand
> To break the blast of winter, stand ;
> And further on, the hoary Channel
> Tumbles a breaker on chalk and sand.

The house is more closely sheltered by fine growths like the Wellingtonia planted by Garibaldi, the great cedar, "sighing for Lebanon," and the grand ilex, also made evergreen by one who was a "lover of trees." For this is Farringford, famous as the home of Tennyson for more than half his life, and the sojourn of so many contemporary celebrities, guests at his house or at his neighbour Mr Cameron's, a retired Indian official, whose wife became so notable

FARRINGFORD HOUSE

Freshwater and the Needles

by her influence over "Alfred," by her unconventionally generous impulses, and by her skill in the then young art of photography. Later on the Camerons disappear from their renowned friend's story, going to die in Ceylon; but all along flit across the page names of renown in both continents, Maurice, Jowett, Sir Henry Taylor, G. F. Watts, Browning, Longfellow, Lowell, O. W. Holmes, and others drawn by the same magnet to this shore.

The mellifluous poet, so dear to his intimates, failed to make himself universally popular in the Island, whose inhabitants were not all able to appreciate him. There is the amusing case of a fly-driver who could not understand the squire of Farringford's greatness. "Why, they only keep one man, and he doesn't sleep in the house!" But that some residents could value their illustrious neighbour is shown by another story of a visitor arriving when the house was in a confusion of unpacking, and being kept waiting in the hall till he was recognised as the Prince Consort.

It is pretty well understood that he who figures too much as an alabaster saint in his official biography, had an earthier side to his nature. His gloomy moods and sensitive shyness sometimes broke out in fits of ill-humour, such as caused Mrs Cameron to remonstrate with him on behalf of a friend of hers found trespassing on his domain, who had come expecting to "see a lion, not a bear." While he shrank in almost morbid horror from

107

peeping pilgrims, he pointed himself out to their gaze
by a picturesque "get up," as to which one of his
favoured grandchildren is said to have bluntly asked
him, "If you don't like people to look at you, why do
you wear that queer hat and cloak?" I have a story
to tell which has not yet, I think, been in print, but
was vouched for by one of those concerned. As
the Poet-laureate, with his friends Palgrave and
Woolner, the sculptor, were walking through a
village, irreverent urchins, having no fear of he- or
she-bears, ran after them with the cry "Old Jew!"
—"Poor Palgrave's nose!" Tennyson whispered to
Woolner, while Palgrave, for his part, presently took
the opportunity of an aside to their companion,
"That's what Tennyson gets by dressing himself up
in such a way!"

Another story of Tennyson's manners reached
me in two pieces, at a long interval, each dovetailing
into each other. I knew a kind and gentle lady
who venerated all genius, and especially his who
was the flower of Victorian literature. Many years
ago she told me, how being invited to see the Uni-
versity boat-race from George Macdonald's house at
Hammersmith, she found herself beside an unknown
gentleman of her own mature age, to whom she
remarked that it would be well if a window could be
opened. He turned his back on her without a word
and walked out of the room, which he would not
enter again. To her dismay, my friend heard that
this was the Poet-laureate, who did not like to be

Freshwater and the Needles

spoken to. She went to her grave hardly able to forgive herself for having unwittingly hurt such a man. Many years afterwards, on his coming to be buried at Westminster, another friend told me how in her girlhood, she was at George Macdonald's boat-race party, when Tennyson was so offended at being spoken to by an old lady, that he shut himself up in a separate room, to which she was sent with some food for him, in the hope that a mere child might be a David to the mood of Saul; and that he spoke very crossly to her because she had forgotten to bring the mustard.

Why tell such tales? it may be asked by those who remember how Tennyson looked forward with horror to his weaknesses being exposed to the public eye. Because a great man's life cannot be kept private; and no picture of him is of value with all the warts painted out. Those who knew the poet agree that he had rough ways and some coarse tastes singularly in contrast with the "saccharinity ineffable" which certain tart critics of another generation distaste in his verse. Those who knew him best are most emphatic as to the essential nobility of character that for them veiled all short-comings. The main interest of his life, as a human document, is that a man who had such faults should by force of genius have been able to transmute them into lessons of purity, courtesy, and charity, that will shine all the brighter as rays of a soul not "faultily faultless, icily regular, splendidly null."

Isle of Wight

And there will be an end to all fruitful biography, if the "good taste" so much admired by this generation is to overlay truth. Who would read the memoirs of a former age if they represented Samuel Johnson as a model of polite elegance, Goldsmith of practical common sense, and Wilkes of untarnished public spirit. So, without wanting in honest admiration for the greatest poet of my time, I protest against the conspiracy of silence by which he has been raised to a House of Lords among the immortals, his old cloak and hat forgotten in ermine and coronet, and his strong tobacco and full-bodied port glorified as nectar and ambrosia.

But if there were some to find the poet no more than a man, and others to regret that he let his world-wide fame be obfuscated in such a title as is sold to a prosperous brewer or money-broker, all tongues are at one in praise of the gentle lady still remembered as a devoted wife, as a friendly neighbour, and as an open-handed mistress of the manor. To William Allingham, Tennyson reported the character given of them by an ex-servant: "She is an angel—but he, why he's only a public writer!" Many a tear was shed when, after long suffering, Lady Tennyson came to rest in the churchyard of Freshwater, her husband lying apart among our renowned dead. Within the Church are memorials of their second son Lionel, whose promising career was cut short by fever in the far East, and he found a hasty grave on a sun-blighted island of the Red Sea.

Freshwater and the Needles

The bard whose "lucky rhymes to him were scrip and share" indeed, while more than one of his publishers dropped off "flaccid and drained," was able later on to build himself a retreat on the Sussex wilds of Blackdown, in a sense even further "from noise and smoke of town." But he still spent part of the year at Farringford; and much of his poetry is coloured by the Isle of Wight scenery, notably *Maud,* that "pet bantling" of his to which early critics were so unkind. Enoch Arden, too, might be thought to have hailed from this shore, but that hazel nuts do not flourish in the Island, unless in the half fossilized form of "Noah's nuts" found in Compton Chine; also, on critical consideration, there appears no long street climbing out of Freshwater, whose "mouldered church," moreover, has been quite masked by rebuilding—but these are poetical properties readily inserted into any picture, such as one that could be taken from a hundred villages on our coast—

> Long lines of cliff breaking have left a chasm;
> And in the chasm are foam and yellow sands;
> Beyond, red roofs about a narrow wharf,
> In cluster; then a moulder'd church, and higher,
> A long street climbs to one tall-tower'd mill;
> And high in heaven behind it a grey down
> With Danish barrows; and a hazelwood,
> By autumn nutters haunted, flourishes
> Green in a cup-like hollow of the down.

Often from these downs, the poet must have watched—

> Below the milky steep
> Some ship of battle slowly creep,
> And on through zones of light and shadow
> Glimmer away to the lonely deep.

111

Isle of Wight

From his own window, he could catch—

> The voice of the long sea-wave as it swelled,
> Now and then in the dim-gray dawn.

And often his steps were turned to that finest scene within an hour's stroll—

> The broad white brow of the Isle—that bay with the coloured sand—
> Rich was the rose of sunset there, as we drew to the land.

On such points of vantage, he was inspired with loyalty and patriotism very different from the feelings of his predecessor in the laureateship, who "uttered nothing base," but who was certainly disposed to frown, when, from the Island cliffs, he saw a British fleet sailing forth against the soon clouded dawn of liberty in France.

Tennyson naturally had a dread of new building about Freshwater; and some other landowners here seem to share the same exclusive spirit, which may account for the neighbourhood not being more "developed" as a resort, while its warmest admirers lament how much it has grown since the Laureate settled here. It has no want of attractions, not always accessible on the steep face of chalk, scarred and pitted by works of time like Freshwater Arch and Freshwater Cave near the little bay, beyond which come honeycombings known by such names as "Neptune's Caves" and "Bar Cave"—"Frenchman's Hole," from an escaped prisoner said to have starved here—Lord Holmes' "Parlour," "Kitchen," and "Cellar," where that governor was in the way

FRESHWATER BAY

of entertaining his friends—" Roe's Hall—" Preston's Bower "—the " Wedge Rock," a triangular mass wedged in between the cliff and an isolated pyramid some 50 feet high — the " Arched Cavern " in Scratchell's Bay, and the " Needles Cave," into which small boats can peep before rounding the jagged corner. It is said that Professor Tyndall used to keep himself in climbing practice by scrambling on these treacherous rocks ; and if this be true, I so far question the wisdom of that pundit. The harrying of airy nests makes a better excuse for such riskful gymnastics. The fissured cliff line is tenanted by sea-fowl, which the report of a gun brings out in screaming and hovering crowds, conspicuous among them the black and white cormorants nicknamed " Isle of Wight parsons."

These sights are to be visited by boat, if a stranger have stomach for the adventure. On foot one can mount the back of the cliff known at first as the Nodes, then as the Mainbench, or in general as the High Downs. At the highest point of the Nodes, nearly 500 feet, the old beacon has been replaced by an Iona Cross in memory of Tennyson, with whom this was a favourite walk in the wildest weather. A grand walk it is upon a crest of greensward so smooth that bicycles find a track here among the flying golf balls. In dry weather this smooth turf is slippery, as one might find too late on its treacherous edges. Further on, the straight way is barred by a fort, where, between Scratchell's

Isle of Wight

Bay and Alum Bay, the ridge narrows and drops to the spur pointed by those insular masses known as the "Needles," that, seen at a hazy distance, rise out of the sea like three castles.

The name of this famous point has been connected with the German *Nieder Fels;* but there seems no need of going further than a homely simile that would come to mind and mouth of sailors who, in another language, have threaded the same suggestion on the southernmost rocks of Africa. Of the three sharp-backed islets that stand out here braving the winds and waves, the innermost is known to have risen 120 feet higher in a tall pillar called "Lot's Wife," which fell in 1784. Since Turner painted them, unless they loomed for him through a haze of imagination, the Needles have dwindled in size. Naturally of course they are worn away by every gale, like their kinsmen "Old Harry and his Wife" on the Dorset coast, one of which isolated masses has been washed down to a stump within the last few years, the same end as threatens the "Parson and Clerk" off the red sandstone cliffs of Devon; and in the far north the more robustly gigantic "Old Man of Hoy" has now but one leg to stand on.

Bitten at as they are by old *Edax Rerum*, the Needles have still a bulk which, dwarfed against the cliffs behind, might not be guessed till one's eyes are fixed upon the lighthouse on the outermost rock, or upon human figures displayed against them, to give their due proportion. Thomas Webster, the geologist,

saw them about a century ago under most
picturesque conditions, when the fifty-gun frigate
Pomone had stuck fast upon the outer edge, and lay
captive there, to be broken up by the next gale, the
waves already spouting through her ports and
hatchways, while all around swarmed a fleet of
smaller vessels engaged in salving the wreck, or
bringing idle spectators to such a singular scene : he
was surprised to find the frigate's hull overtopped by
more than three-fourths of the rock.

On the north side of the Needles opens Alum Bay,
where German visitors will not fail to exclaim
Wunderschòn! and Americans to admire the works
of nature as "elegant!" This famous geological
transformation scene is formed by the Eocene strata
turning up beside the chalk, as at the east end of the
Island, but here with more striking effect, so as to be
a spectacle for the most unlearned eye as well as a
lesson of extraordinary value for those who can read
it, through the manner in which the beds have been
heaved, contorted and thrown into a vertical position
of display. The chalk on one side with its tender
tints is faced on the other by variegated bands of
clay, marl, and sand, the hues of which, after heavy
rain especially, are vivid far beyond our common
experience of the "brown old earth," in some lights
presenting the rainbow of colour described by Englefield, to be so often quoted : "deep purplish-red,
dusky blue, bright ochreous-yellow, grey approaching
nearly to white, and absolute black, succeed each

other, as sharply defined as the stripes in silk; and after rain the sun, which, from about noon till his setting in summer, illuminates them more and more, gives a brilliancy to some of these nearly as resplendent as the high lights on real silk."

His geological ally Webster renders an almost as high-coloured account in more matter-of-fact style. The Alum Bay cliffs, he says,

. . . consist, generally, of a vast number of alternations of layers of very pure clay, and pure sand, with ferruginous sand and shale. Of these beds some are several feet, whilst others are not an eighth of an inch in thickness. Next to the chalk, is a vertical bed of chalk marl; then one of clay of a deep red colour, or sometimes mottled red and white. This is succeeded by a very thick bed of dark blue clay with green earth, containing nodules of marl or argillaceous limestone with fossil shells. Then follows a vast succession of alternating beds of sand of various colours, white, bright yellow, green, red and grey; plastic clay, white, black, grey and red; ferruginous sandstone and shale, together with several beds of a species of coal, or lignite, the vegetable origin of which is evident. The number and variety of these vertical layers is quite endless, and I can compare them to nothing better than the stripes on the leaves of a tulip. On cutting down pieces of the cliffs, it is astonishing to see the extreme brightness of the colours, and the delicacy and thinness of the several layers of white and red sand, shale and white sand, yellow clay and white or red sand, and indeed almost every imaginable combination of these materials. These cliffs, although so highly coloured that they could scarcely come within the limits of picturesque beauty, were not, however, without their share of harmony. The tints suited each other admirably; and their whole appearance, though almost beyond the reach of art to imitate, was extremely pleasing to the eye. Their forms, divested of colour, when viewed near, and from the beach, were often of the most sublime class; resembling the weather-worn peaks of Alpine heights. This circumstance they derive from the same source as those primitive mountains; for the strata being vertical, the rains and snow water enter between them, and wear deep channels, leaving the more solid parts sharp and pointed.

Freshwater and the Needles

The alum that gives the name to this bay, oozing from its motley face, seems no longer of commercial account; but the pure white sand is used in glass-making, and the coloured sands are arranged in fantastic patterns to make curiosities or memorials for the excursionists who flock to this spot by coach, by steamer from Bournemouth and other seaside towns, or by an hour's walk from Freshwater station. For their entertainment, there are two hostelries and some humbler refreshment rooms; but as yet Alum Bay has not been turned into a bathing-place, though round its northern corner rises one of the favourite summer resorts of the Island.

Another contrast appears from the hollow behind the bay. The chalk downs on one side are smooth, as if shaved by their own razor-like edges; on the other, Headon Hill swells up in moorland knolls and banks of heather, its rough sides clothed with tufts of yellow flowerets and ragged grass. Headon Warren is a fitting *alias*. From its blunt head, some 400 feet, we look down upon the lower and darker cliffs of the inner coast, studded with brick forts that would be an ugly sight to an enemy seeking to force the passage of the Solent.

We have done now with wonders, but the north-western face of the Island makes a pleasant shore line, on which, in a mile or so, is reached the snug beach of Totland Bay, the chief bathing-place of this end, all new and smart, its big hotel standing out over the pier, like colonel of a regiment of lodging-houses and villas. Round the next corner comes Colwell Bay, another stretch of sand on which a younger resort is growing up beside crumbling cliffs and tiny chines. At the further horn stands Albert Fort, nicknamed the "brick three-decker," commanding the narrowest part of the Solent, where a long narrow spit from the mainland throws Hurst Castle more than half-way across the three-knot channel, hardly needed as a stepping-stone by any giant who might care to hop over. The next corner, bearing up the Victoria Fort, brings us round to the estuary of the Yar, a stream that shows more estuary than river, opening out with as much complacency as if it drained a basin of ten times three miles. The mouth of this shallow gulf, towards the sea pleasantly masked in woods, is crossed by a causeway leading into Yarmouth.

TOWARD DAY

TOTLAND BAY

YARMOUTH

AMONG its other misfortunes this little Yarmouth
has had that of being over-crowed by the bloated
renown of Great Yarmouth, which trumpets forth many
high notes of interest, from its cathedral-like church
and its ancient "Rows," to its herring fleet and its
Cockney paradises.   The author of *David Copperfield*
himself might not find much to say about the Isle of
Wight Yarmouth, which yet, by its past dignity,
seems to demand a chapter, where it must play at
least the part of text like that blessed word Meso-
potamia.   If we writers might never fill a few pages
without having anything particular to say, what
would become of the circulating libraries?   So let us
see what may be said under the head of Yarmouth,
taken with a stretch of country beyond which deserves
to be better known than it is to the Island visitors.

This little town or big village is best known to
strangers by the pier of the shortest crossing from
Lymington, not indeed the most convenient one, as
there is a gap between the landing and the station,
and trains of the Freshwater line seem to run in no
close connection with the steamers, or make only a

mocking show of connection that adds insult to injury. So one may find oneself stranded here for an hour or two, unless he can go straight on by coach to Freshwater Bay or to Totland Bay, to which also some of the steamers run in the season. But weak-stomached voyagers hail the half-hour's passage as being mostly in the winding mud flats of the Lymington River, with an open prospect towards the Needles, and the low walls of Hurst Castle at the point of its long spit. Hereabouts is the proposed line of a Solent Tunnel which as yet remains in the air, but as a *fait accompli* might lift poor Yarmouth's head, or Totland Bay's, to the height of proud Ryde.

Simple as it stands now, Yarmouth is one of the Island's three ancient boroughs, old enough to have been more than once burned by French excursionists in the bad old days, and a place of comparatively more importance a century ago, when fleets of sails might be wind-bound here for weeks. As bulwark against French and other attacks, a castle was built at the mouth of the Yar, whose remains are now enclosed in the grounds of the Pier Hotel, itself still recalling its state when it was the mansion of Sir Robert Holmes, and entertained Charles II. Else, Yarmouth has not much to boast in the way of architecture, unless some quaint old houses, refreshing after the modernity of Totland Bay. The Church, dating from James I., shows a collection of Holmes' monuments, chief among them a fine statue of Sir Robert Holmes, which had a curious history: it is

YARMOUTH

YARMOUTH

said to have been meant for Louis XIV., but being captured at sea along with the sculptor, he was forced to fit it with a head of Sir Robert. This local worthy, Governor of the Island under Charles II., and a benefactor to the town by embanking its marshy estuary, had a wider renown as one of our early Nelsons; he is repeatedly mentioned in Pepys' *Diary*, and his epitaph tells in sounding Latin how, among other exploits, he more than once beat the Dutch, not always beaten at sea by Charles' sailors, how he took from them the colony of *Nova Belgia*, now better known as New York, and how he captured a cargo of Guinea gold that was coined into a word of much credit in our language.

The Island boasts at least one other sailor as having earned a place in our story. There was a poor tailor's apprentice of Bonchurch who, according to the legend, ran away to the king's navy, proved himself in his first fight worth more than nine men, and rose to be Admiral Sir Thomas Hopson, knighted by Queen Anne for breaking the boom at Vigo. These rough coasts have all along nursed a breed of stout sea-dogs, not always so well employed as in fighting the battles of their country. A century ago Yarmouth, and indeed all this corner, seems to have been a nest of amphibian waiters on the tides of fortune, passing as fishermen plain, but often coloured as smugglers, and proving excellent food for powder when they could be pressed into the navy blue.

Such proof spirits made boon companions for the

eccentric painter George Morland, when in 1799 he fled from London to escape bailiffs. He had thus nearly jumped from the frying-pan into the fire, since at Yarmouth he and his brother were arrested by a party of the Dorset militia on suspicion of being spies for the French—why else should strangers be sketching the coast? At Shanklin, the same suspicion fell upon another artist, whom the fishermen began to pelt from his easel, but he, being a very fat man, cleared himself by patting his paunch, and exclaiming, "Does this look like anything French?" There was a spy-fever all over the Island at that time. In Morland's case, amid the hoots of a patriotic populace, the military Dogberries marched off their prisoners to Newport, where they were discharged by the magistrates only on condition of making no more sketches. In spite of such prohibition, some of Morland's best work represents the Freshwater cliffs and the fishing folk of this coast.

Yarmouth gives itself few seaside airs; yet one has seen bathing-places with no more to build on. There is a stretch of sand where a few bathing-machines are unlimbered; and at low tide the smell of seaweed and salt mud might be considered medicinal. The Pier Hotel (the ex-"George") has recently enlarged itself to invite custom; and on the other side of the pier the Solent Yacht Club makes a showy patch upon a general aspect of well-worn old-fashionedness. If one yearn for a thicker mixture of up-to-date buildings, one has only to take the two or three miles' walk, or few minutes' railway run to Freshwater.

To the east, the Bouldnor estate has been trying to blossom into a red brick resort upon its wooded shore fringed with sand. By the low cliffs on this side we pass on towards the Hamstead Ledges, mines of fossils wealth, which I have heard a British Association President declare to be the most interesting part of the Island; but the general public takes quite an opposite view. The northern shore, with its muddy flats and crumbling banks, has no attraction for the many, till the sands of Gurnard Bay bring us round to the far stretched esplanade of Cowes.

Behind the coast, Parkhurst Forest once extended from Yarmouth to Cowes, where the country is still dotted with its fragments in woods, copses, and straggling hedgerows. Here, between the Downs and the Solent, runs the railway to Newport, keeping well back in the green plain, with more apparent regard for economy of line than for the convenience of the villages it serves on either hand. Its course, indeed, is soon turned inland by the Newton River, whose crops are raised from salterns and oyster-beds, across which the railway gets glimpses of the sea two or three miles away.

Among the branching creeks of this shallow inlet may be sought out Newton, now a mere hamlet, but, in the teeth of its name, boasting itself the oldest borough in the Island, which till not so long ago returned two members of Parliament, among them such celebrities as Churchill, Duke of Marlborough, and George Canning. Though the place has a tiny, tumbledown Town Hall, it was only in the last century that it got a church of its own. But its now larger neighbour Shalfleet, nearer the railway, has one of the most notable churches on the Island, with a massive Norman tower and other relics, such as the rude carving over the north door, the subject of which makes a riddle for antiquaries.

On the opposite side of the line, the pretty village of Calbourne shows another old church, a good deal "restored," to the scandalising of architectural purists; and near it Swainston is one of the most dignified Wight mansions, incorporating the remains of what was once an episcopal palace of the Winchester diocese. One Rector of Calbourne was that Nicholas Udall, now remembered as author of *Ralph Roister Doister*, the first English comedy, but as Headmaster of Eton noted in his own day for out-Heroding the Tudor Herods in school discipline, if Thomas Tusser's experience were not exceptional—whose works the irony of time puts on library shelves beside those of his old tyrant—

> From Paul's I went, to Eton sent,
> To learn straightways the Latin phrase,
> Where fifty-three stripes given to me
> At once I had ;
> For fault but small, or none at all,
> It came to pass, thus beat I was.
> See, Udall, see, the mercy of thee
> To me, poor lad !

SHALFLEET

Yarmouth

The Eton boys who painfully learned to act this Orbilius' comedy, may often have been as sad over it as is the traditional clown in private life. If any of them grew up to be dramatic critics, they might have found some satisfaction in "slating" their ex-master. To us indeed the humours of this farcical piece suggest that our forefathers must have been as easily amused as were Mr Peter Magnus' friends, to Mr Pickwick's thinking. But also a play evidently modelled upon Plautus and Terence, with more than a hint of our old friend *Miles Gloriosus*, is remarkable for keeping in view a motto much neglected by many playwrights, *Maxima debetur puero reverentia*, while indeed it condescends to rough vernacular fun such as might not be expected from that strict disciplinarian, who, after retirement to a country parsonage, ended his days in another mastership at Westminster.

Calbourne one understands to be the "Malbourne" of a novel that made some noise, *The Silence of Dean Maitland*, where this countryside and its people are gauzily veiled under such names as "*Old*port," with its "*Burton's* Hotel," and the "*Swaynestone*" lords of the manor ; while other scenes of this moving story seem better masked as "Chalkbourne" and "Belminster." One rather wonders that novelists think it needful to affect such a thin disguise. In another good story of the Isle of Wight, Mrs Oliphant's *Old Mr Tredgold*, we find the same trick of nomenclature used rather more carelessly, when "Steephill" stands inland from "Sliplin,"

125

and the "*Bunbridge* cliffs" once betray themselves as Bembridge by a slip of the author's pen, or of the printer's eye. We plodding writers of fact are fain to grudge our fanciful brethren such half measures in reality. We would not drive them back upon "the pleasant town of A——" or "the ancient city of B——," all the letters of the alphabet having long ago been used up in this service; but they might be at a little pain of invention to christen their "St Oggs" and "Claverings"; or at least let them be consistent, and not dump down Portsmouth by its honest name, as that first mentioned novelist does, among her ineffectual *aliases*.

Ground so well trodden by honeymooning couples seems to offer a fit stage for fiction; and the Isle of Wight, if it sometimes finds itself called out of its proper names, has less cause to complain of want of appreciation among the novelists who deal with it. Jane Austen only sights it from the walls of Portsmouth, but her interest was in human rather than natural features; and she at least compliments it with its local title "the Island." Mr Meredith coasts or touches its shores here and there, taking such snapshots as :—"The Solent ran up green waves before a full-blowing South-wester. Gay little yachts bounded out like foam, and flashed their sails, light as sea nymphs. A cloud of deep summer blue topped the flying mountains of cloud." Mr Zangwill pushes inland, and writes this testimonial :—"A maze of loveliness, abounding in tempting perspectives.

Yarmouth

Every leafy avenue is rich in promise ; such nestling farmhouses, such peeping spires, such quaint
red tiled cottages, such picturesque old-fashioned
mullioned windows, such delicious wafts of perfume
from the gardens and orchards, such bits of beautiful
old England as are perhaps nowhere else so profusely
scattered!" But another popular novelist, who shall
here be nameless, playing *Advocatus Diaboli* through
the mouth of one of his characters in a perverse
humour, puts the seamy side thus :—"That the Isle
of Wight was only a trumpery toyshop, that its
'scenery' was fitly adorned with bazaars for the sale
of sham jewellery, that its amusements were on a par
with those of Rosherville Gardens ; that its rocks
were made of mud and its sea of powdered lime."

This does not exhaust the catalogue of stories
which have their scene here. Professor Church's
Count of the Saxon Shore and Mr F. Cowper's
Captain of the Wight come rather into the category
of boys' books, the latter being specially well stuffed
with swashing blows and strong "language of the
period." Mr Headon Hill's *Spies of the Wight* gives
a lurid peep into the machinations of a foreign power
against our coast defences, and the tricks of a Fosco-
like villain foiled by one of those Sherlock Holmes
intellects that find it so easy to discover what has
been invented for discovery. We are now approaching the most fashionable resort in the Island, and
there perhaps may come across some of those
scandals and sins of society that give a popular

relish to so much of our circulating literature. Meanwhile, since there is nothing like seeing ourselves as others see us, for a careful picture of Isle of Wight life, let us turn to a French story-teller whose modesty might prefer his name to be withheld.

A collection of novelettes entitled *Amours Anglais,* one of which centres in the Island, is put forth by this writer as an essay in a new school of romance. His preface, dated from "Margate, Isle of Thanet," lets us understand how after long years of sojourn in England he has observed John Bull as closely and profoundly as is possible for a stranger to do, and that he proposes to present English life to his countrymen, stripped of the ridiculous exterior with which it is charged by their caricaturing spirit. This sympathising stranger knows the British soul to be not less interesting and more wholesome than the gloomy and flabby Russian sentiment that has had such a vogue in French fiction. To the facts of *Outre-Manche,* then, he will apply his native "psychologic methods," writing as a Frenchman what he has felt as an Englishman. His aim is "to create an international *genre* of romance, marrying our taste to the humour and the morality of our neighbours. Have I succeeded? The public will judge." So, with the best intentions, our *entente cordialiste* appeals to his French readers. Let the English public now judge.

The heroine of this story is Lilian North, nearly out of her teens, whose home is a cottage wreathed

with ivy and honeysuckle in the outskirts of
Newport. Her father, who "says the service in
the chapel" across the road, is "in orders," not
indeed Anglican orders, he being a fanatical Baptist
who holds that "one is surer of going to hell with the
Archbishop of Canterbury than with the Pope of
Rome himself." Her mother is dead. She has a
married sister not far off at Plymouth—in which,
for once, the author makes a slip, as he evidently
means Portsmouth. Poor Lilian sees almost no
society, except Jedediah, "papa's disciple," a sort
of apprentice minister who "is to read the service
when papa dies." This young colleague and suc-
cessor loves Lilian, with her father's approval; but
she loves him not, as how should she when he has red
eyes, hair of no particular colour, and can talk about
nothing but going to heaven!

Jedediah looks like turning out the hypocritical
villain of the piece. Lilian likes him less than ever
when the hero appears in the person of Harry
Gordon, a young city clerk who has come courting
Miss Arabella Jones, elder daughter of the Baptist
minister at Newport. Mr Jones has the advantage
of his colleague in being a rich man who "preaches
only for his amusement"; and his daughters lead a
rackety life that must have scandalised the connection, especially in the Ryde yachting season, when
they are always at some party of pleasure, "sometimes in a boat, sometimes on horseback, sometimes
in *char-à-bancs*, never knowing in the morning where

they shall lunch in the afternoon, nor where and with whom they shall dance in the evening"; and when they visit Newport it is with a train of ever fresh cavaliers.

At a picnic in the ruins of Carisbrooke, Lilian makes the acquaintance of Harry Gordon, whom her friend Arabella Jones professes to disdain as a shy awkward boy. But Lilian takes to him, and Harry begins to pay more attention to her than to the proud Miss Jones. At a game of blindman's buff among the ruins, the blindfolded hero is more deliberate than need be in pawing over Lilian's face and figure before giving her name. Cupid catches them both.

Another day there was a party to Freshwater, where the sea is always *méchant*, even in fine weather. The ladies having ventured out in a boat, found themselves in such danger that they were glad to get on shore. Then Arabella put her backward swain to the test with the question—"if we had gone down, which of us would you have saved first?" Harry did not answer, but his looks were on Lilian, to the spiteful displeasure of Miss Jones. So, in talking of a ball about to be given by the wealthy Baptist pastor of Ryde, she scornfully bid Lilian come to it only if properly dressed—"none of your shabby dyed frocks and halfpenny flowers!"

Lilian's cheeks glowed with shame under this insult, and she took the first opportunity of stealing away to weep all alone by moonlight. But Harry, indignantly sympathetic, had followed her, guided by her sobs. In vain she bid him return to his Arabella. Arabella indeed! He had never much cared for Miss Jones, whom he now detested after such an exhibition of ill-natured rudeness. As they strolled on the Freshwater esplanade, Lilian's foot slipped; and Harry, holding her up, took the opportunity to clasp the heroine in his arms. They went back an engaged couple—*cela va sans dire.*

The courtship had to be done on the sly; yet the young couple must have attracted suspicion in any more censorious neighbourhood, such as that not far away, which we hear of, on good authority, as bubbling over with "gossip, scandal, and spite." Every day Harry rode from Ryde to Newport, met at her garden-gate by Lilian, to keep company with all the freedom of a British maiden and of an innocent heart. "I gave sugar to his horse, which was called Fly; we picked flowers, and ran races against each other." Only the jealous Jedediah guessed what was going on. When Harry entered the house, he feigned great attention to the religious exhortations of the father, but could not make way in his good-will, while Jedediah scowled at every sight of his rival, whose ring Lilian wore "hidden under my mitten," yet not perhaps from that green-spectacled monster.

Autumn broke up the gay non-conformist society of the Island. The Misses Jones went off to make fresh conquests at Brighton. Harry had to go back to his London office, but every week-end he took a bed at the "Bugle" Hotel of Newport, spent Sunday with his *fiancée's* family, and returned to business by the last train. In spite of this breaking of the Sabbath, the Baptist minister believed that the young man came all the way from London to hear him preach. But at last the neighbours began to talk; so the lovers saw themselves obliged to meet only in secret, and to pour out their hearts in long letters. The worst of it was that Harry grew cross and impatient. His father, a rich shipowner at Cardiff, would never consent to his engagement with the daughter of a poor Baptist preacher. If he knew, he would cut his son off with a shilling, "as the law authorises him to do." The Rev. Mr North, for his part, would frown on his child's union with a family far from sound in faith. Lilian was for a long engagement, in hopes that the old people would come round. Harry's more heroic remedy was an immediate secret marriage such as, in tale and history, has sooner or later the effect of forcing parents to make the best of a bad business. The wooer becomes ill-temperedly pressing; Lilian at length consents; but when these unpractical youngsters lay their heads together, they run up at once against the serious difficulty of finding a minister to marry them. Then the heroine takes the desperate resolution of throwing herself upon the generosity of her unsuccessful suitor. She leads Jedediah into the garden; and now for a scene in the best style of French fiction.

Yarmouth

"Do you love me, Mr Jedediah?" I said.

The poor fellow had a moment of joy and hope.

"I ask if you love me well enough to wish my happiness, even if that should cause you pain?"

"Yes," said he, all at once overcast again.

"And do you feel yourself capable of doing all you can to aid the accomplishment of what will be grievous to you?"

"Perhaps," replied Jedediah with a sigh.

"Mr Jedediah, I love Harry Gordon."

"I feared so!"

"I wish to marry him."

"And you reckon on me to win the consent of Mr North. But nothing will move him, Miss Lilian: he has discovered that Mr Harry's father is a Puseyite, and his aunt a nun in Ireland. His conviction is that Mr Harry is a treacherous foe who has got into intimacy with him for the purpose of stealing his papers and spying upon his conduct. Nothing will move him!"

"I am aware of it, so I have made up my mind to marry without his knowledge."

"Without his knowledge! But who will marry you?"

"You, Mr Jedediah!"

"Me!"

"Yourself, my good, my dear Jedediah!"

"But," went on Jedediah, after a moment's consideration, "even if I were weak enough to consent to so culpable an action, such a union would not be valid in the eye of the law. Not being a member of the Established Church, I cannot celebrate a civil marriage. You must go before the Registrar; and, as you are both under age, this official will not marry you without your father's authorisation in writing."

"Alas! what are we to do?"

Jedediah reflected.

"What would you say if I undertook to get this authorisation for you?"

"I should say that you are our good angel."

"Then, let me manage."

I held out my hand and he kissed it. His glasses were moist with tears.

Three days later, he brought me the document which I required. He was very pale. I would have asked questions, but he let me

133

understand that he would not answer. "I have done wrong for your sake, Miss Lilian," he said.

I learned afterwards that he had procured my father's *blanc-seing* under pretext of a petition addressed to the Government against the Ritualists, and especially against the use of surplices, baldaquins over altars, and confessionals.

I do not know to what stratagems Harry had recourse for obtaining the necessary papers. What is certain is that we were married on Easter Tuesday, before the Registrar of the county, after which Jedediah gave us the nuptial benediction in a little chapel of the Baptist communion situated in the environs of Plymouth (*Portsmouth*). He married us without looking at us. I have never seen a scene more strange, nor a man more unfortunate.

He refused to come and share the wedding-cake with us, which we ate at my sister's.

But those English love-marriages between rash young people by no mean always end in living happily all the rest of their days; and the story soon turns tragic, its scene shifting from the Island. After that secret wedding, Harry returns to London, leaving his wife in an awkward position, where Jedediah is her only comfort. Love still blinds her eyes to the selfishness of Harry; but the reader sees how she might have been better off with poor Jedediah, who is not such a villain after all, but only the Dobbin or Seth Bede of the tale. The time comes when her marriage can no longer be hidden. Harry takes lodgings for her in London at the house of a Mrs Benson, whose husband, being employed at the Bricklayers' Arms Goods Station, finds it convenient to live in a four-roomed house in Shoreditch, too large for a quiet couple.

To this sympathetic landlady, Lilian relates the

foregoing story, with many tears and gulps of *tisane*, a refreshment, it seems, known to Shoreditch sick-beds. Her child is born dead. The young mother in her feverish weakness fancies that Jedediah has revengefully contrived some defect in the ceremony, and cries out to have her marriage made legally complete at the parish church. Harry, moved by her delirium, writes to both parents, confessing the truth. A curate is sent for, who politely but hastily says a few prayers at the sick-bed, then hurries off to a tea-party at the West-end. Lilian dies the same night. Harry weeps, to be sure, but soon grows tired of sitting up with the dead, and comes down to smoke a pipe with the landlord.

Next day Gordon *père* arrives in a great rage, but, at the sight of his dead daughter-in-law, he is touched to the point of taking off his hat, as English gentlemen, it appears, will do on such special occasions. Mr North, on his arrival, shows natural grief, which is soon turned to wrath by the sight of a crucifix laid on his daughter's breast, contrary to "the statute of the fifteenth year of Elizabeth," as he knows well; and he gives up all hope of her eternal welfare, on hearing how her last moments had been corrupted by the prayers of an Anglican priest. Mrs Benson, who takes that wide view of religion spread in France by such divines as the Savoyard Vicar and such poets as Beranger, in vain tries to comfort him.

"What! Is she lost for such a small matter?

Isle of Wight

The curate did not stay ten minutes. I know nothing about any of your sects; but I am sure that there is only one *bon Dieu* for all of us; and Benson thinks so too."

Jedediah's grief is not less deep but more reasonable. It is he who performs the service when, on a snowy evening, Lilian is buried in Bethnal Green Cemetery.

But the sensational story has a cynical epilogue. Kind Mrs Benson, *qui sent son Dickens*, never forgets her young lodger. One Sunday, as her husband is reading *Lloyd's News*, which he spells out conscientiously from the "*premier Londres* of M. Jerrold to the last line of the advertisements," he exclaims at a paragraph stating that a clergyman, named North, formerly of the Isle of Wight, had been caught trying to break images over the altar of Exeter Cathedral, and sent to an asylum as a madman. Nothing is heard of Jedediah, and we can only trust that he duly succeeded to the Newport pastorate and found some consoling helpmeet in the congregation. Of Harry there is no news till some years later, when the Bensons go to Cardiff to meet a married daughter returning from New Zealand. Calling at the Gordons' house, they learn that the father is dead, and that Harry, now his own master, is about to marry a Miss Jones of Ryde, not indeed the proud Arabella, but her younger sister Florence, to whom time has transferred his facile affections.

The last scene introduces Miss Florence going

over the house soon to be her own, and finding in a drawer an old black glove torn and soiled. Harry denies all knowledge of it, but when his new beloved proposes to throw it away, he shows that it has some value for him. The suspicious damsel sulks, plays off on his jealousy a cousin in the Scots Greys, refuses to waltz with her *fiancé*, except at the price of his giving up that glove. He sighs as a widower, but obeys as a wooer. Giving one secret kiss to poor Lilian's glove, he resigns it to the triumphant Miss Jones, who flings it on the fire, and holds out her white fingers for the forgiven Harry to kiss, yet not without a smiling stab at that unknown rival's memory—"Her hand was larger than mine!"

Now for the moral of this realistic romance. "Let him who has never committed a cowardice of the kind, who has never sacrificed a memory to a hope, the forgotten love to the fresh one, the dead to the living, let him cast at Harry the first stone!" To which poor Jedediah will not say *Amen*.

The latest scene for fiction set in the Isle of Wight —*All Moonshine*, by Richard Whiteing—is no photograph of actual society like that just reduced, but a most imaginative romance, not to say a wild nightmare inspired by the dangers of over-population, and based on the statistical claim quoted in my first chapter, that the world's eighteen hundred millions or so could all find room to meet in this Island. The author, falling asleep at Ventnor, dreams of such a universal rendezvous as coming about in the form of astral bodies from all ends of the earth, when some very strange things happen among the unsubstantial multitude. At one moment it seems as if the ghostly armies of England and Germany were about to close here in a lurid Armageddon ; but they are fain to fraternise before the general peril of an earthquake announced at Shide as threatening to crack the globe and overwhelm civilisation in waves of fire let loose from hell. The dreamer awakes to find the world what it is, with nations and classes seeking to fatten on their neighbours' poverty, kings and statesmen watching each other's armaments in mutual suspicion, priests hoisting flags on their churches in exultation over the slaughter of fellow-Christians, and only an unpractical poet or romancer to cry here and there—

> Ah ! when shall all men's good
> Be each man's rule, and universal peace
> Lie like a shaft of light across the land,
> And like a lane of beams athwart the sea,
> Thro' all the circle of the golden year.

CALBOURNE

COWES

WE now come to one of the most important places in the Island, a place that holds up its double head for second to none in the way of dignity and fashion, though it began life as two small castles built by Henry VIII. at the Medina's mouth to protect the harbour of Newport.

> The two great Cows that in loud thunder roar,
> This on the eastern, that the western shore,
> Where Newport enters stately Wight.

" I knew when there was not above three or four houses at Cowes," says Sir John Oglander, who yet had counted three hundred ships at anchor there ; "and I was and am persuaded that if our wars and troubles had not unfortunately happened, it would have grown as famous as Newport." Another scourge of the Island in his time was the activity of lawyers to stir up strife, whereas the first attorney who ventured himself here had been ignominiously charivaried out of this Arcadian scene by order of the Governor. But it might be, he admits, that lawyers were no more to blame than the absence of ships of war, once such good customers for the

139

Islanders' produce. "Now peace and law hath beggared us all, so that within my memory many of the gentlemen and almost all the yeomanry are undone." One observes the distinction drawn by this rule of thumb economist between the ruinous effects of civil war and the profitable accidents of helping to ruin another country.

It is easy to understand how Cowes came to be the Tilbury and Gravesend of Newport, then by and by to supplant it as the Island's chief port. In the days of small vessels, such a harbour as Newport offers was roomy and accessible enough, while it had the advantage of being more out of the way of hostile attack. London, Glasgow, Newcastle, Exeter, Bristol are only a few examples of great ports lying some way up navigable rivers; then on the larger scale of the world, one at once thinks of Calcutta, Canton, Montreal, New Orleans, Rosario, and so on. Some of these inland havens have kept their commercial position only by pains and cost hardly worth while to save half-a-dozen miles of water carriage; so, as ships grew too big for the tiny wharves of Newport, they would unload at the mouth of the river that makes the one good harbour on the Island. Thus Cowes grew apace; and a century ago it bid fair to be at least the second Wight town, till Ryde took a sudden start in prosperity. Like Ryde and Yarmouth it throve by victualling the great war fleets and convoys that often lay windbound in the Solent. But Cowes got a special string to its

Cowes

bow in the ship-building industry rooted here, then another in its position as headquarters of Solent yachting; and royal favour went to bring it into fashion. There was a time when it aspired to be a mere Margate or Sandown, in honour of which a Georgian poet named Jones is moved to predict—

> No more to foreign baths shall Britain roam
> But plunge at Cowes and find rich health at home!

To tell the truth, Cowes hardly shines in this capacity. Its bathing is not everywhere safe in the currents of the Solent; and to pick out a sandy oasis on the rough beach one must go eastward towards Gurnard Bay. Nowadays, indeed, the place is so spoilt by the patronage of European royalties and American millionaires, that it does not much care to lay itself out for the holiday-making *bourgeois* and his olive branches. The straggling town, divided by the Medina, has no particular charm unless that of a marine flavour. It is far from being so picturesque as Ventnor, or so imposing as Ryde; and apart from the artificial beauties of the parks enclosing it, its surroundings are commonplace beside those of Newport. Its main interest is on the sea-face looking over the shallow waters of the Solent, beside which East Cowes huddles along a narrow main street, that winds up and down, in and out, here and there, making a quaint show of houses old and new, half and half, dwellings mixed with shops, an unusual proportion of them providing refreshments, when they do not display such wares as ship's lanterns, and other sea-fittings from cordage to carronades. The central point is the steamboat pier opposite the station; then further west comes the Victoria Pier with its pavilion, on a scale that shows how little Cowes cares to cater for your common Saturday to Monday visitor.

Cowes makes the Mecca of the yachtsman, as St Andrews of the golfer. It is the most famous station of those idle craft that in our day diverge into two different forms—the steam vessels, models of comfort and elegance, even luxury, some of them fitted for making pleasure-cruises all over the world; and the mere sailing boats, that seem utterly useless but as racing machines to skim like butterflies over some quiet sea, with their decks as often as not half under water—"a sort of metal torpedo with two or three balloons fixed on to it." This is a pastime as expensive as the turf, and sometimes as unsatisfactory to the amateurs who seek social glory thereby. Not all the gentlemen who swagger about in blue jackets here are so much at home on the ocean wave as for the nonce they would fain appear. Not all those big and smart craft so much admired in the roads of Cowes are very familiar with the breeze or the billow of the open sea. The sailing masters and crews of some of them must have a good easy time of it; and one suspects they prefer being in the service of a fine-weather sailor, whose purse is his main quali-fication for seamanship, to taking orders from some old salt who knows the ropes as well as they do. We remember Jack Brag and his skipper Bung. But there are yachtsmen of another school, whose blood has the salt in it that goes so far to make England what it is, men who, without having the means to own idle vessels, dearly love playing the mariner in good earnest, and can spend no happier holiday than in working some small craft with their own hands, taking rough and smooth as it comes, getting health and pleasure out of return for a month or so to something like the old Viking life, and all its tingling charm of a struggle with the forces of nature. Sailors of this stamp can here buy or hire craft of all kinds, but perhaps more cheaply at other ports on the Solent, for it is not only at regatta-time that Cowes has a name for high charges.

The Solent with its almost landlocked waters, its many creeks, and its havens of refuge never more than a few miles off, makes a good cruising-ground for small craft such as can be sailed by the owner with the help of one or two hands working for love or money. Yet there are special difficulties here in the broken shore-line, the shifting banks, the shallows, and the treacherous currents, that call for some nautical ability, and even local experience to interpret the many buoys and beacons marking the channels of a watery labyrinth. The chief danger, apart from an occasional rough sea and squalls to be looked out for through openings in the land, is the violence of the tides, that encounter one another from each end of the Solent, so as to produce the peculiar result of a double high water—the ebb, after an hour or so, being driven back up to Southampton by a fresh flow.

There are, of course, various yacht clubs that take the Solent for their province ; but the admiral of them all is the " Squadron," one of the most exclusive clubs in the world, whose members have the much coveted right to fly St George's white pennant on their yachts, and other privileges. Its membership is the port for which some of the most sumptuous yachts are fitted out. Many a millionaire would give a large slice of his fortune for admission to this body ; but ill-gotten gold that buys titles, social advantages, and lordly yachts, is not an *Open Sesame* here ; and there are aspirants who know, like Spenser, what it is in this matter "to have thy Prince's grace and want *his* peers'." Princely, royal or imperial patronage is seldom wanting for the regatta at the beginning of August, with which, passing on to the coast from Goodwood, the fashionable world disperses itself for the season in the blaze of fireworks that marks the end of "Cowes week." During this week, Cowes becomes the focus of "smart" society, money and champagne flying over it like sea spray, and all its accommodation crammed ; indeed, it would have no room for half its visitors, if not a few of them did not bring their own quarters in the shape of the innumerable yachts that by day are radiant with rainbow bunting, and by night illuminate the waters of the

YACHTING AT COWES

A. HEATON COOPER

Cowes

Solent with thousands of lights. It is said indeed that, of late years, yachting begins to decline in fashion; that the expensive craft are allowed to take longer holidays, and that "Cowes week" is not filled with such a cloud of canvas. It may well be that our "smart set" find the winds and waves disturbing to the calculations of Bridge.

During Cowes' water-carnival, some of the finest yachts afloat may still be seen at anchor off the R. Y. S. Clubhouse, standing out prominently on the sea-front, with its flagstaff and jetty, at which only members and officers of the navy are privileged to land, under the muzzles of a miniature battery brought from Virginia Water for holiday service. This building, whose glass gallery is the grand stand of yacht racing, has been adapted from the old castle of Henry VIII., in the seventeenth century used as a state prison. Here Sir William Davenant spent his hours of confinement in writing an heroic poem, *Gondibert*, which one fears to be hardly read nowadays, unless it makes part of prison libraries. There are some score cantos of it, filling eight score or so of folio pages; and this, as in the contemporary case of the bear and the fiddle, brings the story only to the middle, for as the author puts it in metaphors readily suggested at Cowes, "'tis high time to strike Sail, and cast Anchor (though I have run but half my Course) when at the helm I am threatened with Death, who, though he can visit us but once, seems troublesome, and even in the Innocent may beget such a gravity as diverts the Musick of Verse."

The parade of Cowes runs on beyond the castle, past gardened villas, to open out as the Green, a strip of sward set with seats that make the pit of the open-air theatre for which the Solent is stage in its yacht-racing season. At the end of this is the point marked by a brick ivy-clad mansion called Egypt, why so called, one knows not, unless that the name, occurring elsewhere in England, seems sometimes connected with gipsy memories. Did one wish to go gipsying, this end of Cowes was once fairly well adapted for such purposes; but cottages of gentility keep on spreading along the sea edge.

At Egypt is the bathing beach, from which the sea wall extends onward towards a bank of wild shrubbery called the "Copse," a miniature Under-cliff, where, rooted in singularly tenacious mud, an almost impassable jungle offers scope for the adventurous imagination of youth. This is skirted by a rough path above the shore, where at morn and eve may be seen flesh and blood *replicas* of Frederick Walker's "Bathers," or of Mr Tuke's "August Blue" scene, exhibited "without the formality of an apparatus," as the Oxford man in *Humphrey Clinker* has it. As for the bathing-machines further back, a guide-book of his generation states that "from the manner in which they are constructed, and the position they occupy, a person may safely commit himself to the bosom of Neptune

at almost any state of the tide." Yet one may hint
to strangers not desirous of committing themselves
to Abraham's bosom, that the currents run strong
here, and that some parts of the shallow shore deepen
suddenly.

One of the sandiest bathing-places on this shore
is at Gurnard's Bay, about two miles along, which
has an hotel of its own and other beginnings of
a seaside resort. This used to be a landing-place
from the mainland; and here was the site of
another Roman villa. The guide-books of a future
generation may have more to say about Gurnard's
Bay; but I must ask the reader now to turn back
to Cowes.

At the back of the town is its Church, built in the
time of the Commonwealth, that did not much foster
church architecture; and behind this stands the
manorial mansion of Northwood Park in somewhat
gloomy grounds opened by funereally classical gates.
The older parish church is that of Northwood, some
way inland, which itself, in its day, had been an
offshoot of Carisbrooke. Northwood Park hived for
a time the foreign nuns who lately swarmed to other
quarters at Ryde. This mansion had long been
looked on by true blue Protestants as a half-way
house to Rome, when it was the home of William
George Ward, a prominent name in the "Oxford
Movement" that so much shifted the Anglican
establishment's centre of gravity. He went over to
the Roman Church, and moved to another house

near Totland Bay, where his neighbour Tennyson
had warm words to say over his grave—

> My friend, the most unworldly of mankind,
> Most generous of all ultramontanes, Ward,
> How subtle at tierce and quart of mind with mind,
> How loyal in the following of thy Lord!

The chief hotels and lodging-houses are found on
that part of the parade east of the "Squadron,"
which at one time occupied the Gloucester Hotel.
The crooked main street leads us to the river suburb
of Mill Hill, and to the floating bridge by which the
Medina is crossed to East Cowes. There has been
talk of a tunnel here, as under broader channels; but
the amphibious folk of this port are still content with
their ferry.

East Cowes, though at one time the more important side, has long been eclipsed by its western
neighbour. It may be described as a suburb of
ambitious roads mounting the wooded background
from a rather mean frontage, so as to bring
into curious juxtaposition some characteristics
of Norwood and Rotherhithe. At the seaward
end it has a short esplanade of its own, from which
is to be had a fine sunset view over the Solent. The
old fortress on this side has entirely disappeared.
The most interesting house here is Slatwoods, the
boyhood's home of Dr Arnold of Rugby, his father
having been collector of customs at this port. Arnold,
born in a house at West Cowes now marked by a
tablet, but brought up on the other side, always had

OSBORNE HOUSE

an affection for Slatwoods, and slips of its great willow tree were transplanted to his successive homes at Laleham, Rugby, and Fox How.

East Cowes is shut in by the grounds of East Cowes Castle and Norris Castle, mansions of the modern Gothic period, that have had noble occupants and royal guests. Norris Castle, at the point of the estuary open to briny breezes from every quarter, was in 1833 tenanted by the Duchess of Kent, sea-air having been ordered for her daughter's precious health. The Princess Victoria made here a collection of sea-weeds which she presented to her friend Maria da Gloria, the girl-queen of Portugal ; and no doubt in this sequestered nook she was able to go about more freely than at Bognor or Brighton. She seems to have much enjoyed her stay on the Solent, probably then taking a fancy to this neighbourhood, which in later life led to the purchase of Osborne, her favourite residence when Balmoral was too bleakly bracing. The park begins beyond the ascent out of East Cowes, extending along the wooded northern shore towards the small inlet called King's Quay, that pretends to be a landing-place of King John, who, after signing Magna Charta, is dubiously said to have sulked here among the pirates of the Island.

Osborne Manor, whose name has been clipped to so aristocratic a sound, would have been originally no more than an *Austerbourne* or *Oyster-bed*, that, from the Bowermans, an old Island family not yet extinct, came to belong to one Eustace Mann, who, during the troubles of the Civil War, is supposed to have buried a mass of gold and silver coins in a coppice still known as Money Coppice, and having forgotten to mark the spot, was never afterwards able to recover his treasure. Had it been found in the course of the last half century, a curious lawsuit might have arisen between the rights of the Crown and of the Queen as private owner. By marriage the estate came into the hands of the Blachfords. From Lady Isabella Blachford it was purchased by Queen Victoria in 1840, who enlarged her property here to an area of upwards of 5000 acres, bounded north by the Solent, south by the Ryde and Newport road, east by the inlet of King's Quay, and west by the Medina.

The Blachford mansion, spoken of a century ago as one of the largest and best in the Island, gave place to the palace of Osborne, royally adorned with pictures and statuary, that turns its Palladian face to the Solent, while from the road behind only the flag tower and campanile can be seen peeping above the rich foliage of the park. A "Swiss Cottage" contained the model dairy and kitchen, where the princesses are understood to have been instructed in housewifely arts, and a museum of curiosities collected by the princes in their travels through an empire on which the sun never sets. At Barton Manor-house, a picturesque old mansion added to the estate and adapted as residence of the steward,

was the Prince Consort's home-farm, which "a Mr
Wilkinson, a clergyman" is quoted in guide-books
as praising for a model of all that could be done to
make the best of a naturally poor soil. The late
Queen's love of seclusion prompted her to increase
and enclose her demesne, till she could drive for miles
in her own grounds, kept strictly private during the
royal residence.

Behind Osborne, overlooking the Medina, is
Whippingham Church, whose parish takes in
Osborne and East Cowes, as West Cowes was a
dependent on Northwood. This church, sometimes
attended by the royal family, is rich in mortuary
memorials, among them Theed's monument of the
Prince Consort, placed here by "his broken-hearted
and devoted widow, Queen Victoria," and the chapel
that is the tomb of Prince Henry of Battenberg,
married in Whippingham Church, 1885. The structure, finely situated, has a singularly un-English look,
its German Romanesque features understood to have
been inspired by the taste of the Prince Consort, on
which account her late Majesty's loyal subjects would
fain have admired the effect, as many of them could
not honestly do. A wicked tale is told of a gentleman well known in the architectural world, who, on
a visit at Whippingham, was surprised by a sum-
mons to Osborne. Unfortunately, this stranger had
not been furnished with a *carte du pays*, and when
the Queen led the conversation to Whippingham
Church, asking advice what should be done with it,

he bluntly gave his opinion : " The only thing to be done, madam, is to pull it all down ! "—whereupon the uncourtly adviser found his audience soon brought to an end.

Other stories or legends are locally current, illustrating the difficulties of etiquette that hampered her Majesty's desire to be on friendly terms with her less august neighbours. One hears of guests scared off by the sight of a red cloth on the steps to mark how royalty would be taking tea or counsel within ; and of others suddenly bundled out of the way, when the Queen's unpretentious equipage was announced as approaching. It seems that majesty's neighbours were not all neighbourly. A lady of title here is said to have closed her gates to the Queen's carriage, which never again took that direction. Such an assertion of private rights would have astonished that high-titled Eastern potentate, of whom it is told that, being entertained at the seat of one of our greatest dukes, he advised the then Prince of Wales to have their host executed without delay as much too powerful a subject !

After the death of Queen Victoria, the present Sovereign gave up this estate to be in the main a public memorial of her, though Osborne Cottage is still occupied by the Princess Henry of Battenberg, Governor of the Island with which she has so many happy and sorrowful associations. The palace has been in part adapted as a home for convalescent officers, the room in which the Queen died and other

WHIPPINGHAM CHURCH.

apartments being kept as used by her, to make a sight at present open on certain days. In the grounds are the new buildings of a Naval College, whose cadets will be brought up in view of the famous anchorage haunted by memories of our "wooden walls," and often stirred by the mighty machines that have taken their place, we trust, to the same good purpose.

Of all the naval pageants these shores have beheld, none could be more impressive than when, that dull winter afternoon of 1901, stirred only by tolling bells and booming minute guns, the body of Europe's most venerated Sovereign was borne across the Solent through a mile-long lane of British and foreign war-ships, on her last journey to Windsor.

THE GATES OF THE ISLAND

BEFORE turning away from the Solent, we may take a look at its northern shores, and the mainland ports making gateways of the strait and island that serve their populations as playground.

Cowes lies opposite Southampton, with which it has direct communication up the long inlet of South-ampton Water, the least expeditious passage to the Island, but the pleasantest in fine weather, most of the hour's voyage being by that wooded arm of the Solent, where on one side stretch the heaths and copses of the New Forest's Beaulieu corner; while the other is broken by the mouths of the Hamble and of the Itchen. Between these creeks, stands conspicuous the Netley Hospital, said to be the longest building in England, overshadowing Netley Castle, adapted as a modern mansion, and the picturesque old ruins of Netley Abbey, fallen to be a junketing resort for Southampton. The Royal Victoria Hospital, a name well earned by the late Queen's interest in it, was built for soldiers invalided in the Crimean War, and became to our army what the Haslar Hospital, at Gosport, is to the navy.

The Gates of the Island

Netley Bay is now headquarters of the Motor-Yacht Club, housed in an ex-Admiralty yacht.

Too many of the Isle of Wight passengers who embark or land at Southampton Pier, know not what a mistake they make in hurrying on without a look at one of the most interesting old towns in England, which from the railway or the docks may appear to be no more than one of its most prosperous ports. The Northam and Southam of early days have here grown into a still growing municipality, whose lively streets imbed some most notable fragments of the past, now reverently preserved. The largest portion of the walls is a stretch of curious archways facing the west shore, behind which filthily picturesque slums have been cleared away and replaced by a pile of model lodging-houses that our era of sanitation puts in bold contrast with the Middle Ages. These Arcades, as they are called, seem to have been the defensible entrances to a line of mansions, very eligible for their period. Behind, beside the spire of Southampton's oldest church, is a Tudor house said to have accommodated Henry VIII. and Anne Boleyn on their brief honeymoon. The oldest of the houses on the sea front, by the "King's Quay" as it used to be called, is believed to have been tenanted by King John, perhaps by Henry III. ; and among the many King John's lodges and King John's palaces scattered over England, this seems to have the best right to the honour thus claimed for it.

Isle of Wight

Further on, near the end of the pier, is the West Gate, under which Henry V.'s men-at-arms and archers clanked out on their way to Agincourt.

> Suppose that you have seen
> The well-appointed king at Hampton pier
> Embark his royalty, and his brave fleet
> With silken streamers the young Phœbus fanning :
> Play with your fancies, and in them behold
> Upon the hempen tackle ship-boys climbing ;
> Hear the shrill whistle which doth order give
> To sounds confused ; behold the threaden sails,
> Borne with the invisible and creeping wind,
> Draw the huge bottoms through the furrowed sea,
> Breasting the lofty surge : O do but think
> You stand upon the rivage and behold
> A city on the inconstant billows dancing ;
> For so appears this fleet majestical,
> Holding due course to Harfleur.

Such a floating city as Shakespeare saw here in his mind's eye, would seem but a hamlet beside the streets of craft from all the world that now crowd Southampton docks. Behind them, near the foot of High Street, is a building which, if tradition lie not, may boast itself the oldest house in England, for, stable as it is now, it sets up to be a remnant of King Canute's residence, who on the shore hereabouts, perhaps enacted his famous scene of commanding the waves, more effectually restrained by the heroes of modern industry ; but on that oft-told tale Leslie Stephen drily remarks, "that an anecdote is simply the polite name of a lie."

From the Quay quarter, what a well-known novelist styles the "brightest, airiest, lightest, prettiest

The Gates of the Island

High Street in England," leads up to the Bargate, imposing survival of mediæval architecture, with which Southampton is proud to hamper her busy main thoroughfare, long after prosaic Londoners have banished their obstructive Temple Bar. The long street, hence known as "Above Bar," goes out between pleasant parks, then as a lordly avenue that begins one of the finest high-roads in the kingdom, running on to Winchester. As this avenue is approached, on the left stands a building that should be viewed with grateful respect by all conscientious tourists and their guides, since it is the headquarters of the Ordnance Survey maps. Further on, beside the road, is reached Southampton Common, one of the prettiest natural parks and playgrounds at the gate of any great town, seeming to be, what indeed it is, a half cleared bit of the New Forest.

The woods of the New Forest come within a few miles of Southampton, which has other pleasant scenes about its salubrious site on a gravelly spit projecting between the Itchen and the Test, angling streams of fame. Its sea-front on the West Bay is hardly an admirable point unless at high water, as it more often shows a green expanse of slime and malodorous weed that by no means *ladet zum Baden*, fit rather for the paddling of adventurous mud larks. But the citizens, more ingenious than Canute, catch the elusive tide in a basin that makes an excellent open-air swimming bath. The strong smell of sea-weed is offensive to some strangers, who may comfort themselves by considering it as wholesome : had this rubbish bank been German, it would probably be utilised for some sort of *Kur*, with a three weeks' course of sanatory sniffs, and a *Nach-kur* of whey treatment in the Isle of Wight. Southampton had once indeed a chalybeate spa of its own, to which its Victoria Rooms seems a monument.

This old seaport has had notable sons, from Isaac Watts, whose statue in the park looks down on a flower-bed visited by busy bees, to Charles Dibdin, whose nautical songs were not so well adapted to the restraint of angry passions. If all tales be true, its oldest celebrity is that Bevis of Hampton, whose story, indeed, inconvenient critics father upon a twelfth century French romance ; and it has certainly been told in several languages : so far off as Venice, this widely popular hero is found figuring as a sort of local Punch. But for the confusion of all who doubt his Hampshire origin, the name Bevis Mount still preserves on the Itchen bank the memory of a stronghold he threw up here against the Danes ; and who was he if not Bevis of Hampton ? The story also gives him a connection with the Isle of Wight ; so, as we began with dull history, let us draw towards an end with a taste of what, one fears, must count rather as fiction, perhaps expanded about some core of legendary fact.

Sir Bevis of Hampton was one of the favourite romances of the feudal age ; and his adventures were familiar to John Bunyan's unregenerate youth, if

The Gates of the Island

little known to the Southampton boys who in our time pass the sixth standard, however well versed they may be in our own "penny dreadful" literature. Yet *Ivanhoe*, *Pathfinder*, and the *Three Musketeers* rolled into one, would make a tame hero beside Sir Bevis. As became a hero, he had difficulties to contend with all along, the first being an unnatural mother who, one grieves to say, was a Scottish princess. Married to Guy, Earl of Southampton, whose name suggests some connection with the still more famous lord of Warwick, she preferred a foreign prince, Sir Murdour, a name that gives plain hint of his nature, as well as a dim anticipation of David Copperfield's tyrant.

Guy being betrayed by his wife and slain by her paramour when Bevis was only seven years old, the wicked pair's next object would naturally be to get rid of a child who might avenge his father. With a fortunate want of wisdom often shown by the bad characters of romance, the mother did not see to this business herself, but charged it on Saber, the child's uncle, by whom he had been reared ; then the kind Saber, as proof of compliance, sent her his nephew's princely garments sprinkled with the blood of a pig, while he kept the boy safe and sound, disguised as a shepherd. But Bevis had too high a spirit to await the opportunity of revenge promised by his uncle when he should come to manhood. Feeding his sheep on the downs, he became so infuriated by the sounds of revelry in which his mother and her new husband sought to drown the memory of their crime, that he burst into the hall, knocking down the porter who would have shut him out, unpacked his young heart of its indignation before the whole company, and with three blows of a "mace" laid his stepfather senseless before them all. Thus did this seven-year-old princeling show a resolution that might well put Hamlet to shame; and as he was so terrible with a stick, we may guess what feats he would perform when it got to sword-play.

The guilty mother was so much displeased by such conduct, that she punished her precociously brave child by sending him to be sold for a slave in heathen lands. Thereby he came into the hands of a Saracen king named Ermyn, whose daughter, Josyan, at once fell in love with the young captive, according to the romantic precedent followed in such cases down to the days of Pocahontas. Ermyn, too, recognising the boy's quality at a glance, proposed to make him his heir and son-in-law on condition of his abjuring Christianity. But the heroes of old were as orthodox as gallant. Bevis, though not yet in his teens, lifted up such a bold testimony against the errors of Mahound, that the king saw well to drop the subject, and for the present took him on as page, promising him further advancement in the course of time. Still no amount of friendly intercourse with unbelievers could shake the youngster's faith. He had reached the age of fifteen, when certain Saracen knights rashly ventured to touch on his religion, whereupon he slew them all, some sixty or so, with remarkable ease. Ermyn forgave him for this once, and Josyan with kisses and salves soon cured him of his wounds ; then, in return for their kindness, he obligingly rid them of a fearful wild boar that had long been the terror of the country.

These petty exploits had made merely the work of our hero's 'prentice hand ; the time was now come for him to be dubbed a knight, presented on the occasion with a marvellous sword called " Morglay," and the best horse in the world, by name " Arundel." Ermyn had soon need of a peerless champion. Bradmond, King of Damascus, was demanding Josyan's hand, with threats to lay waste the land if his suit were refused ; but a lad of mettle like Bevis, of course, found no difficulty in laying low that proud Paynim and all his host. Josyan was so lost in admiration of such prowess, that she proposed to her Christian knight after a somewhat unmaidenly fashion ; but Bevis would give her no encouragement till, for his sake, she professed herself ready to renounce the Moslem faith.

But when the king heard how his daughter was being converted to Christianity, his patience came to an end. Not daring to use open violence against the invincible youth, he sent him on an embassy to King Bradmond, his late adversary, who at the point of Bevis' sword had lately sworn to be Ermyn's vassal, and was now commanded, on his allegiance, to secure the bearer of the sealed letter which Bevis carried to his own destruction. The author of *Hamlet* may have taken another hint from this incident. But our impetuous knight needed no treacherous credentials to get him into trouble. At Damascus he found a crowd of Saracens worshipping an idol, which his sound principles moved him to knock over into the mud with proper contempt : the Mohammedans, whatever their doctrinal shortcomings might be, were, as a matter of fact, strongly set against idolatry, but Christian minstrels allowed themselves a poetical license on such points. King Bradmond and all his men, backed by the fanatical population of Damascus, were odds too great even for a pious hero. Bevis, fairly overpowered for once, was thrown into a dungeon with two ravenous dragons to keep him company. It was only a matter of some twenty-four hours' combat for him to kill the dragons with the butt-end of a staff that came to his hand ; but hunger proved a sorer enemy. Now we have the two most familiar lines of this long poem, as quoted in *King Lear*—

> Rats and mice and such small deer,
> Were his meat for seven long year.

At the end of seven years, he escaped by something like a miracle, and after visiting Jerusalem, rode off to Josyan, whom he found still faithful to him at heart, though formally the bride of an outrageous heathen, the King of Mounbraunt. To his castle Bevis proceeded, not without blood-curdling adventures on the way, and introduced himself as a poor palmer, welcomed for the sake of her Christian lover by Josyan, though she did not recognise him so soon as did his good horse Arundel, that in its vehement excitement at his voice outdoes the fidelity of Argus; then his springing on its back without touching a stirrup reveals him like the bending of Ulysses' bow. Having got the king out of the way by means of a somewhat unchivalrous fib, Bevis and Josyan eloped together, meeting encounters which showed how little his long imprisonment had unsteeled the paladin's sinews. His first feat was to kill a brace of lions at one blow; and next he fell in with a giant named Ascapard who, wounded all over his thirty feet of length, was glad to save his life by becoming Bevis' page.

It was now high time for our hero to be turning homewards. Several years back, before his imprisonment, he had casually fallen in with one of his cousins, sent to search him out and bring him to the immediate assistance of his uncle Saber, who had fled to the Isle of Wight for refuge from the tyrant Murdour. As the first stage of his journey, Bevis proceeded by sea to Cologne, where the bishop happened to be another uncle of his, so he took the opportunity to have Josyan and Ascapard christened, the latter behaving most irreverently under the rite, so as to play the part of a mediæval gargoyle in the edifying story. The bishop, for his part, used the opportunity of having such a champion at hand to destroy a fiery dragon that infested the country ; and in return for this service of some little difficulty, equipped Sir Bevis with a hundred knights, at the head of whom he landed in Hampshire, leaving Josyan at Cologne with Ascapard in attendance.

Under an assumed name, so grown and sun-tanned that his own mother treated the stranger politely, he now introduced himself into the house of Sir Murdour, undertaking to serve him against Saber, but playing a trick on him in the way of carrying off his best horses and arms to the enemy. Before coming to an end with that caitiff, however, Bevis had to return to Cologne to rescue Josyan from certain perils she had got into through her devotion to him ; then at last they both joined his uncle in the Isle of Wight. The local Macbeth's fate now drew to its fifth act. In vain he summoned to his aid both a Scotch and a German army. When he had to do with such prodigies of strength as Bevis and Ascapard, Murdour could expect nothing but to be overthrown, captured, and boiled into hounds' meat in a great caldron of pitch, brimstone, and lead, as duly befell at Carisbrooke. His wicked wife, hearing how it had fared with him, very properly threw herself from the top of a high tower. His triple army had no more fight in them after the death of their leader, and the delivered citizens of Southampton hailed with joy their true lord, who at last thought himself entitled to wed Josyan after so long and chequered a courtship.

But the author of this long poem is not yet out of

The Gates of the Island

breath, and he still takes his hero through what may be called an appendix of adventures, in which Bevis once more goes abroad. King Edgar's son so much admired Arundel's form in a horse-race at court, that he tried to steal this peerless steed, and was kicked to death in the stable for his pains. The angry father was for having the horse's master hanged; but the barons got him off with exile. While wandering homeless, his wife presents him with twin sons, as fresh hostages to their troubled fortune. Ascapard now turns unfaithful, and steals Josyan from him to restore her to her Saracen husband; but after a separation of seven years or so all comes right again, unbelievers and traitors are duly slain as they deserve, and Bevis meets no further check in his triumphant career of baptising heathen lands in blood, if not otherwise. Meanwhile, in his absence, King Edgar spitefully did him further wrong by confiscating the family estate, which the nephew had handed over to Saber. This injury must be redressed by a visit of Bevis to London, where his exploits seem hardly historical. He had now two sturdy sons to back him up, and these being chips of the old block, they easily contrived to kill sixty thousand people in a battle fought about Cheapside and Ludgate Hill, which brought the king to a reasonable mood.

> So many men at once were never seen dead,
> For the water of Thames for blood wax red
> From St Mary Bowe to London Stone.

In short, one of Bevis' sons won the crown of England, with the hand of its heiress; the brother was provided with a kingdom abroad; and Bevis himself returned to another of his foreign dominions, to live happily ever afterwards till, at a good old age, he, Josyan, and Arundel died within a few minutes of each other, the knight and his true lady sumptuously buried in a church, where even his dead body continued to work miracles.

> Thus ended Bevis of Hampton
> That was so bold a baron.

Have I said enough to persuade strangers that they are wrong in not stopping at Southampton on a visit to the tourist-haunted Island? To Americans this port should be of special interest, as hence sailed the *Mayflower* and the *Speedwell*, freighted with the hopes of a New England, but the smaller vessel proving unseaworthy, the adventurers, all packed on board the *Mayflower*, finally embarked at Plymouth, which thus gets credit for the departure of an expedition that really set out from Delft Haven, winged by the parting charge of its large-minded pastor. I had the pleasure of recommending a stay at Southampton West to Mr W. D. Howells, who in a recent book owns to having enjoyed it; and indeed there is more to be seen and enjoyed in or about Southampton than at many places better famed in the tourist world.

On the west side of Southampton Water, through

outskirts of the New Forest, is soon reached the Boldre River, near the mouth of which stands Lymington, a town before mentioned as pier of the shortest crossing to the Island, at its Yarmouth end, where it has been proposed to make a tunnel from the spit on which Hurst Castle rises. Of Lymington there is not much else to be said, but that it has a look of having come down in the world, its trade of shipbuilding not being what it once was, though the estuary still makes a station for yachts. From the open sea it is separated by flats, that were utilised as salterns. The scenery in the background is more taking, where the edge of the New Forest plantations is soon reached over the heathy swells of Sway Common.

Westward, the crumbling cliffs of the coast are fringed by groups of hotels and lodging-houses growing along Christchurch Bay to Highcliffe Castle, which was recently selected as *Kur-ort* for the Kaiser, who here seems to have profited by the mild air and by the views of the Isle of Wight that are the chief attraction of this shore. He may also have admired the prospect on Hengistbury Head, which some stories make the scene of the first German invasion of England. Then beyond the mouth of the Stour and Avon, are reached the purlieus of Bournemouth, where the Island drops out of sight.

On the other side, between Lymington and South-ampton Water, extends to the Solent a heathy projection of the New Forest, not so much known to strangers as it deserves. The centre of interest here is the ruined Beaulieu Abbey, from the materials of which Henry VIII. is said to have built Hurst Castle, while its foundation is the one good deed recorded of King John, and that wrung out of him with as much pain as was Magna Charta. The legend goes that this graceless king, bearing a grudge against the Cistercian Order, had persuaded or compelled its abbots to attend a parliament at Lincoln, where he threatened to fling them under the feet of wild horses. But at night he was terrified by a dream : brought to trial before a nameless judge, with the churchmen he had menaced for witnesses against him, he found himself condemned to a severe scourging at their hands, like his father's chastisement for the death of Thomas à Becket. And lo! when he awoke, the lashes had left no visionary smart. So he saw wise to make expiation for the sacrilege he had meditated ; then his repentance took the established form of building and endowing a Cistercian Abbey at Beaulieu. The remains still make a hoary show by the Beaulieu River, further down which Buckler's Hard was once a building place of men-of-war ; and at the mouth was an old ferry to the Island. There is not much traffic now about this muddy shore, near which, towards Lymington, Sowley Pond takes rank as the largest Hampshire lake. The Solent, here locked in by the Isle of Wight, has the aspect of a great lake in

The Gates of the Island

views that Cobbett took to bear out the title *Bellus locus*, vernacularly corrupted into *Bewley*. And, as I have given a catalogue of novels dealing with the Island, let me mention an excellent one, Mr A. Marshall's *Exton Manor*, which clearly has for its scene this edge of the New Forest.

The chief Solent ferry is, of course, at Portsmouth, whereof tourists might do well to see more than is seen from the railway line to its pier, the main knot of Isle of Wight communications, while by Gosport and Southsea, on either side of the town, are alternative crossings to Ryde. Portsmouth is not so rich in antiquities as Southampton, its most notable buildings being the fine modern Church of Portsea, one of the grandest town-halls in England, and the largest Naval Barracks in the world; but it is an ancient place, interesting as our chief marine arsenal, which in case of war might become a Sebastopol or a Port Arthur. Like Plymouth, it is rather a group of towns, Portsmouth, Portsea, and Southsea, run together beside the wide inlet of the harbour, on the other side of which stands Gosport. Naturally it has a marked naval flavour, strongest on the Hard, familiar to so many generations of Jacks and Sues, behind which the narrow main street of Landport makes such a lively scene of a Saturday night. Off Gosport Hard is moored the old *Victory*, whose deck no Briton can tread without pride, nor would a generous enemy be unmoved on the spot where "mighty Nelson fell," and in the gloomy cockpit

169

where he died. Portsmouth has for another shrine the birthplace of Charles Dickens, at No. 387 Commercial Road, Landport, now cared for as public property and containing a collection of relics. Walter Besant was also a native, who has celebrated the scenes of his boyhood in *Celia's Arbour*.

The great sight is the Dockyard, over which all visitors who can glory in the name of Briton are conducted by its garrison of Metropolitan Police; but foreigners must bring special credentials for admission. A visit to the *enceinte* of fortifications cannot be recommended, as these are of a modestly retiring disposition, and make a purposed blank on the faithful Ordnance Survey maps. Beyond the fort-crowned Downs behind, some fine country may be reached by tram; but the scenery of the low island on which Portsmouth has its site, too much consists of bastions, barracks, prisons, and other useful, but unlovely institutions.

Southsea, the moral West End of Portsmouth, which is at its east end, holds out most attractions to tarrying strangers. It seems a favourite place of residence or sojourn for retired or idle officers of both services, who enjoy the stir of parades and regimental bands, and the view of the Solent always alive with yachts, steamers, and men-of-war; but it is not so well adapted for a quiet family bathing-place, unless to the taste of nursery maids, who here would be well off for red-coated and blue-jacketed "followers." A special feature is the wide Common cutting off the

The Gates of the Island

houses from the sea-front, with its gay piers and long esplanade leading round the modernised walls of Southsea Castle. Hence let us take our last gaze upon the wooded shores of the Isle of Wight, where, four or five miles off across the Solent, Ryde steeple stands up as the starting-point of our arm-chair tour, now to be ended, I trust, with the reader's gratuity of good-will towards his *cicerone*.

INDEX

173

Index

Index

Index

PRINTED BY OLIVER AND BOYD, EDINBURGH

BLACK'S BEAUTIFUL BOOKS

ALL WITH FULL-PAGE ILLUSTRATIONS IN COLOUR

By Post, Price 20s. 6d.   ## THE **20s.** NET SERIES   Size 9 × 6¼ ins.

Algeria and Tunis
Painted and Described by FRANCES E. NESBITT. 70 Full-Page Illustrations in Colour.

The Alps
Described by SIR MARTIN CONWAY. Painted by A. D. M'CORMICK. 70 Full-Page Illustrations in Colour.

Ancient Tales and Folk-Lore of Japan
By R. GORDON SMITH, F.R.G.S. Painted by Japanese Artists. 57 Full-Page Illustrations in Colour.

Australia
Painted by PERCY F. S. SPENCE. Described by FRANK FOX. 75 Full Page Illustrations in Colour.

Belgium
Painted by A. FORESTIER. Described by G. W. T. OMOND. 77 Full-Page Illustrations in Colour.

Birds of Britain
By J. LEWIS BONHOTE, M.A., F.L.S., F.Z.S. 100 Full-Page Illustrations in Colour, selected by H. E. DRESSER.

Birket Foster
By H. M. CUNDALL, I.S.O., F.S.A. 100 Full-Page Illustrations (over 70 in Colour) and many Sketches in the Text.

Burma
Painted and Described by R. TALBOT KELLY, R.B.A. 75 Full-Page Illustrations in Colour.

Cambridge
By M. A. R. TUKER. Painted by WILLIAM MATTHISON. 77 Full-Page Illustrations in Colour.

Canada
Painted by T. MOWER MARTIN, R.C.A. Described by WILFRED CAMPBELL. 76 Full-Page Illustrations in Colour.

The Channel Islands
Painted by HENRY B. WIMBUSH. Described by EDITH F. CAREY. 76 Full-Page Illustrations in Colour.

The Clyde
Painted by MARY Y. HUNTER and J. YOUNG HUNTER. Described by NEIL MUNRO. 67 Full-Page Illustrations in Colour.

Constantinople
Painted by WARWICK GOBLE. Described by PROF. ALEXANDER VAN MILLINGEN, D.D. 63 Full-Page Illustrations in Colour.

From Damascus to Palmyra
By JOHN KELMAN, M.A., D.D. Painted by MARGARET THOMAS. 70 Full-Page Illustrations in Colour.

Egypt
Painted and Described by R. TALBOT KELLY, R.B.A. 75 Full-Page Illustrations in Colour.

Egyptian Birds
Painted and Described by CHARLES WHYMPER, F.Z.S., B.O.U. 51 Full-Page Illustrations in Colour.

Happy England
By HELEN ALLINGHAM, R.W.S. Text by MARCUS B. HUISH. 80 Full-Page Illustrations in Colour. (Size 9½ × 7 ins.)

The Rivers and Streams of England
Painted by SUTTON PALMER. Described by A. G. BRADLEY. 75 Full-Page Illustrations in Colour.

English Costume
By DION CLAYTON CALTHROP. 73 Full-Page Illustrations in Colour and numerous Sketches in the Text.

The English Lakes
Painted by A. HEATON COOPER. Described by WILLIAM T. PALMER. 75 Full-Page Illustrations in Colour.

Essex
Painted by BURLEIGH BRUHL, R.B.A. Described by A. R. HOPE MONCRIEFF. 75 Full-Page Illustrations in Colour.

Florence and some Tuscan Cities
Painted by COLONEL R. C. GOFF. Described by MRS. GOFF. 75 Full-Page Illustration in Colour.

The Flowers and Gardens of Japan
Painted by ELLA DU CANE. Described by FLORENCE DU CANE. 50 Full-Page Illustrations in Colour.

The Lake of Geneva
Painted by J. HARDWICKE LEWIS and MAY HARDWICKE LEWIS. Described by FRANCIS GRIBBLE. 60 Full-Page Illustrations in Colour.

Greece
Painted by JOHN FULLEYLOVE, R.I. Described by REV. J. A. M'CLYMONT, M.A., D.D. 75 Full-Page Illustrations in Colour.

Kate Greenaway
By M. H. SPIELMANN, F.S.A., and G. S. LAYARD. 75 Full-Page Illustrations (51 in Colour) and numerous Illustrations in the Text.

Hampshire
Painted by WILFRID BALL, R.E. Described by REV. TELFORD VARLEY. 75 Full-Page Illustrations in Colour.

Holland
By NICO JUNGMAN. Text by BEATRIX JUNGMAN. 75 Full-Page Illustrations in Colour.

The Holy Land
Painted by JOHN FULLEYLOVE, R.I. Described by REV. JOHN KELMAN, M.A., D.D. 93 Full-Page Illustrations, mostly in Colour.

Hungary
Painted by MR. AND MRS. ADRIAN STOKES. Described by ADRIAN STOKES, A.R.A. 75 Full-Page Illustrations in Colour.

India
By MORTIMER MENPES. Text by FLORA A. STEEL. 75 Full-Page Illustrations in Colour.

Ireland
Painted by FRANCIS S. WALKER, R.H.A. Described by FRANK MATHEW. 77 Full-Page Illustrations in Colour.

The Italian Lakes
Painted by ELLA DU CANE. Described by RICHARD BAGOT. 69 Full-Page Illustrations in Colour.

Japan
By MORTIMER MENPES. Transcribed by DOROTHY MENPES. 100 Full-Page Illustrations in Colour.

Kashmir
Described by SIR FRANCIS EDWARD YOUNGHUSBAND, K.C.I.E. Painted by MAJOR E. MOLYNEUX, D.S.O. 75 Full-Page Illustrations in Colour.

Kent
By W. TEIGNMOUTH SHORE. Painted by W. BISCOMBE GARDNER. 73 Full-Page Illustrations in Colour.

Familiar London
Painted by ROSE BARTON, A.R.W.S. 61 Full-Page Illustrations in Colour.

London to the Nore
Painted and Described by W. L. WYLLIE, R.A., and MARIAN AMY WYLLIE. 60 Full-Page Illustrations in Colour.

London Vanished and Vanishing
Painted and Described by PHILIP NORMAN, F.S.A. 75 Full-Page Illustrations in Colour.

The Scenery of London
Painted by HERBERT M. MARSHALL, R.W.S. Described by G. E. MITTON. 75 Full-Page Illustrations in Colour.

George Morland
By SIR WALTER GILBEY, Bt. 50 Full-Page Reproductions in Colour of the Artist's best work.

Naples
By AUGUSTINE FITZGERALD. Described by SYBIL FITZGERALD. 80 Full-Page Illustrations in Colour.

The Royal Navy
Painted by NORMAN WILKINSON. Described by H. LAWRENCE SWINBURNE. 61 Full-Page Illustrations in Colour.

New Zealand
Painted by the brothers F. and W. WRIGHT. Described by THE HON. W. P. REEVES, Lately High Commissioner for New Zealand. 75 Full-Page Illustrations in Colour.

Oxford
Painted by JOHN FULLEYLOVE, R.I. Described by EDWARD THOMAS. 60 Full-Page Illustrations in Colour.

John Pettie
By MARTIN HARDIE, B.A., A.R.E. 50 Full-Page Illustrations in Colour and 8 in Black and White.

PUBLISHED BY A. AND C. BLACK · SOHO SQUARE · LONDON · W.
AND OBTAINABLE THROUGH ANY BOOKSELLER AT HOME OR ABROAD

BLACK'S BEAUTIFUL BOOKS

By Post, Price 20s. 6d.   THE **20s. NET** SERIES (*continued*)   Size 9 × 6¼ ins.

The Riviera
Painted and Described by WILLIAM SCOTT. 75 Full-Page Illustrations in Colour.

Rome
Painted by ALBERTO PISA. Text by M. A. R. TUKER and HOPE MALLESON. 70 Full-Page Illustrations in Colour.

Bonnie Scotland
Painted by SUTTON PALMER. Described by A. R. HOPE MONCRIEFF. 75 Full-Page Illustrations in Colour.

The Savage South Seas
Painted by NORMAN H. HARDY. Described by E. WAY ELKINGTON, F.R.G.S. 68 Full-Page Illustrations in Colour.

Northern Spain
Painted and Described by EDGAR T. A. WIGRAM. 75 Full-Page Illustrations in Colour.

Southern Spain
Painted by TREVOR HADDON, R.B.A. Described by A. F. CALVERT. 75 Full-Page Illustrations in Colour.

Surrey
Painted by SUTTON PALMER. Described by A. R. HOPE MONCRIEFF. 75 Full-Page Illustrations in Colour.

Sussex
Painted by WILFRID BALL, R.E. 75 Full-Page Illustrations in Colour.

Venice
By MORTIMER MENPES. Text by DOROTHY MENPES. 100 Full-Page Illustrations in Colour.

Warwickshire
Painted by FRED. WHITEHEAD, R.B.A. Described by CLIVE HOLLAND. 75 Full-Page Illustrations in Colour.

Wessex
Painted by WALTER TYNDALE. Described by CLIVE HOLLAND. 75 Full-Page Illustrations in Colour.

Yorkshire
Painted and Described by GORDON HOME. 71 Full-Page Illustrations in Colour.

By Post, Price 10s. 6d.   THE **10s. NET** SERIES   Size 9 × 6¼ ins.

Bruges
And West Flanders
Painted by A. FORESTIER. Described by G. W. T. OMOND. 37 Full-Page Illustrations in Colour.

The Light Side of Egypt
Painted and Described by LANCE THACKERAY. 36 Illustrations in Colour, Cloth (album shape). Size 10½ × 8 ins.

A Book of Porcelain
Painted by WILLIAM GIBB. Text by BERNARD RACKHAM. 30 Full-Page Illustrations in Colour of Selected Examples in the Celebrated Collection of the Victoria and Albert Museum, London. (Size Crown Quarto).

The Highlands and Islands of Scotland
Painted by WILLIAM SMITH, Jun. Described by A. R. HOPE MONCRIEFF. 40 Full-Page Illustrations in Colour

From Sketch=Book and Diary
By LADY ELIZABETH BUTLER. 28 Full-Page Illustrations in Colour and 21 Line Drawings in the Text by LADY BUTLER.

By Post, Price 7s. 11d.   THE **7s. 6d. NET** SERIES   Size 9 × 6¼ ins.

Abbotsford
Painted by WILLIAM SMITH, Jun. Described by REV. W. S. CROCKETT. 20 Full-Page Illustrations in Colour.

Adventures among Pictures
By C. LEWIS HIND. 24 Full-Page Illustrations (8 in Colour and 16 in Black and White).

Alpine Flowers and Gardens
Painted and Described by G. FLEMWELL. 20 Full-Page Illustrations in Colour.

The Beautiful Birthday Book
By GERTRUDE DEMAIN HAMMOND, R.I. 12 Full-Page Illustrations in Colour. Decorative Borders by A. A. TURBAYNE.

Brabant & East Flanders
Painted by A. FORESTIER. Text by G. W. T. OMOND. 20 Full-Page Illustrations in Colour.

British Floral Decoration
By R. F. FELTON, F.R.H.S., F.N.C.S., etc. (Florist to the late King Edward VII. and many Courts of Europe). 28 Full-Page Illustrations (12 in Colour).

William Callow
By H. M. CUNDALL, I.S.O., F.S.A. 22 Full-Page Illustrations in Colour and Numerous Illustrations in the Text.

Canterbury
By W. TEIGNMOUTH SHORE. Painted by W. BISCOMBE GARDNER. 20 Full-Page Illustrations in Colour.

Chester
Painted by E. HARRISON COMPTON. Described by FRANCIS DUCKWORTH. 20 Full-Page Illustrations in Colour.

A History of the Church of England
By J. F. KENDALL, M.A. Illustrated from Autochromes of the Church Pageant taken by ERNEST C. ELLIOTT. 24 Full-Page Illustrations (16 in Colour).

Country Sketches for City Dwellers
By MRS. WILLINGHAM RAWNSLEY. 16 Full-Page Illustrations in Colour.

Dutch Bulbs & Gardens
Painted by MIMA NIXON. Described by UNA SILBERRAD & SOPHIE LYALL. 24 Full-Page Illustrations in Colour.

Edinburgh
Painted by JOHN FULLEYLOVE, R.I. Described by ROSALINE MASSON. 21 Full-Page Illustrations in Colour.

English Costume
Painted and Described by DION CLAYTON CALTHROP. In Four Sections, each containing 18 to 20 Full-Page Illustrations in Colour, and many Illustrations in the text: Section I. Early English—II. Middle Ages—III. Tudor and Stuart—IV. Georgian, etc. Price 7s. 6d. net each.

Eton
Painted by E. D. BRINTON. Described by CHRISTOPHER STONE. 24 Full-Page Illustrations in Colour.

Eton from a Backwater
(Portfolio)
Painted by H. E. LUXMORE. 12 Coloured Plates.

Gardens of England
Painted by BEATRICE PARSONS. Described by E. T. COOK. 20 Full-Page Illustrations in Colour.

The Garden that I Love
By ALFRED AUSTIN (*Poet Laureate*). Painted by GEORGE S. ELGOOD, R.I. 16 Full-Page Illustrations in Colour.

The Charm of Gardens
Text by DION CLAYTON CALTHROP. 32 Full Page Illustrations in Colour (Size 9½ × 7 ins.).

Geneva
Painted by J. HARDWICKE LEWIS and MAY HARDWICKE LEWIS. Described by FRANCIS GRIBBLE. 20 Full-Page Illustrations in Colour.

Grouse and Grouse Moors
Painted by CHARLES WHYMPER, F.Z.S. Text by GEORGE MALCOLM and CAPTAIN AYMER MAXWELL. 16 Full-Page Illustrations in Colour (Size Large Crown 8vo.).

PUBLISHED BY A. AND C. BLACK · SOHO SQUARE · LONDON · W.

ALL WITH FULL-PAGE ILLUSTRATIONS IN COLOUR

By Post, Price 7s. 11d.   **THE 7s. 6d. NET** SERIES (*continued*)   Size 9×6¼ ins.

Haunts of Ancient Peace
By ALFRED AUSTIN (*Poet Laureate*).
Painted by AGNES LOCKE. 20 Full-
Page Illustrations in Colour.

The Heart of Scotland
Painted by SUTTON PALMER. Described by A. R. HOPE MONCRIEFF.
24 Full-Page Illustrations in Colour.
(Size 10¼×7½ ins.)

Inns of Court
Painted by GORDON HOME. Des-
cribed by CECIL HEADLAM. 20 Full-
Page Illustrations in Colour.

Isle of Man
Painted by A. HEATON COOPER.
Described by W. RALPH HALL CAINE.
20 Full-Page Illustrations in Colour.

Isle of Wight
Painted by A. HEATON COOPER.
Described by A. R. HOPE MONCRIEFF.
24 Full-Page Illustrations in Colour.

Lamia's Winter Quarters
By ALFRED AUSTIN (*Poet Laureate*).
Painted by GEORGE S. ELGOOD, R.I.
16 Full-Page Illustrations in Colour,
and 13 Head and Tail Pieces by
WILLIAM SCOTT.

Lausanne
Painted by J. HARDWICKE LEWIS
and MAY HARDWICKE LEWIS.
Described by FRANCIS H. GRIBBLE.
24 Full Page Illustrations in Colour.

Letters from the Holy Land
By LADY BUTLER, Painter of "The
Roll Call." 16 Full-Page Illustrations
in Colour by LADY BUTLER.

Liége and the Ardennes
Painted by G. F. FORESTIER. Des-
cribed by G. W. T. OMOND. 20
Full-Page Illustrations in Colour.

London
Text by A. R. HOPE MONCRIEFF.
32 Full-Page Illustrations in Colour
(Size 9½×7 ins.).

The Tower of London
Painted by JOHN FULLEYLOVE, R.I.
Described by ARTHUR POYSER. 20
Full-Page Illustrations in Colour.

Flowers and Gardens of Madeira
Painted by ELLA DU CANE. Des-
cribed by FLORENCE DU CANE. 24
Full-Page Illustrations in Colour.

Malta
Painted by SIGNOR V. BORON. Des-
cribed by FREDERICK W. RYAN. 20
Full-Page Illustrations in Colour.

Middlesex
Painted by JOHN FULLEYLOVE, R.I.
Described by A. R. HOPE MONCRIEFF.
20 Full-Page Illustrations in Colour.

Montreux
Painted by J. HARDWICKE LEWIS.
Described by FRANCIS H. GRIBBLE.
20 Full-Page Illustrations in Colour.

Moscow
Painted by F. DE HAENEN. Described
by HENRY M. GROVE (H.M.'s Consul
at Moscow). 32 Full-Page Illustrations (16 in Colour).

The New Forest
Painted and Described by MRS.
WILLINGHAM RAWNSLEY. 20 Full-
Page Illustrations in Colour.

Nuremberg
Painted by ARTHUR GEORGE BELL.
Described by MRS. A. G. BELL. 20
Full-Page Illustrations in Colour.

The Rubáiyát of Omar Khayyám
Translated by EDWARD FITZGERALD.
Painted by GILBERT JAMES. Edited,
with notes, by REYNOLD ALLEYNE
NICHOLSON, M.A. 16 Full-Page Illus-
trations in Colour. (Size 10¼×7½ ins.)

Pompeii
Painted by ALBERTO PISA. Described
by W. M. MACKENZIE, M.A., F.S.A.
24 Full-Page Illustrations (20 in
Colour).

St. Petersburg
Painted by F. DE HAENEN. Des-
cribed by S. DOBSON. 32 Full-Page
Illustrations (16 in Colour).

Scottish Life and Character
Painted by H. J. DOBSON, R.S.W.,
A.R.C.A. Described by WILLIAM
SANDERSON. 20 Full-Page Illus-
trations in Colour.

Our Life in the Swiss Highlands
By JOHN ADDINGTON SYMONDS and
his daughter MARGARET. Painted
by J. HARDWICKE LEWIS. With a
Preface by MRS. VAUGHAN (MAR-
GARET SYMONDS). 22 Full-Page
Illustrations (20 in Colour).

The Homes of Tennyson
Painted by HELEN ALLINGHAM,
R.W.S. Described by ARTHUR H.
PATERSON. 20 Full-Page Illustra-
tions in Colour.

Days with Velasquez
By C. LEWIS HIND. 24 Full Page
Illustrations (8 in Colour and 16 in
Black and White).

Westminster Abbey
Painted by JOHN FULLEYLOVE, R.I.
Described by MRS. A. MURRAY SMITH.
21 Full-Page Illustrations in Colour.

Winchester
Painted by WILFRID BALL, R.E.
Described by the REV. TELFORD
VARLEY, M.A., B.Sc. 24 Full-Page
Illustrations in Colour.

Windsor
Painted by GEORGE M. HENTON.
Described by SIR RICHARD RIVINGTON
HOLMES, K.C.V.O. 20 Full-Page
Illustrations in Colour.

Worcestershire
Painted by THOMAS TYNDALE. Des-
cribed by A. G. BRADLEY. 24 Full-
Page Illustrations in Colour.

The Wye
Painted by SUTTON PALMER. Des-
cribed by A. G. BRADLEY. 24 Full-
Page Illustrations in Colour.

Yorkshire
Coast and Moorland Scenes
By GORDON HOME. 31 Full-Page
Illustrations in Colour.

Yorkshire
Dales and Fells
Painted and Described by GORDON
HOME. 20 Full-Page Illustrations in
Colour.

Yorkshire
Vales and Wolds
Painted and Described by GORDON
HOME. 20 Full-Page Illustrations
in Colour.

By Post, Price 6s. 4d.   **THE 6s. NET** SERIES   Size 7½×5¼ ins.

The Cotswolds
Painted by G. F. NICHOLLS. Des-
cribed by FRANCIS DUCKWORTH. 24
Full-Page Illustrations in Colour.

The Upper Engadine
Painted by J. HARDWICKE LEWIS.
Described by SPENCER C. MUSSON.
24 Full-Page Illustrations in Colour.

Galloway
Painted by JAMES FAED, Jun. Des-
cribed by J. M. SLOAN. 24 Full-Page
Illustrations in Colour.

Ireland
Painted by FRANCIS S. WALKER,
R.H.A. Described by FRANK MA-
THEW. 32 Full-Page Illustrations in
Colour.

Jamaica
Painted by A. S. FORREST. Des-
cribed by JOHN HENDERSON. 24
Full-Page Illustrations in Colour.

Kew Gardens
Painted by T. MOWER MARTIN,
R.C.A. Described by A. R. HOPE
MONCRIEFF. 24 Full-Page Illustra-
tions in Colour.

Liverpool
Painted by J. HAMILTON HAY.
Described by WALTER SCOTT. 25
Full-Page Illustrations in Colour.

The Norwegian Fjords
Painted and Described by A. HEATON
COOPER. 24 Full-Page Illustrations
in Colour.

Paris
By MORTIMER MENPES. Text by
DOROTHY MENPES. 24 Full-Page
Illustrations in Colour and numerous
Line Illustrations in the Text.

The Peak Country
Painted by W. BISCOMBE GARDNER. Des-
cribed by A. R. HOPE MONCRIEFF. 24
Full-Page Illustrations in Colour.

Tyrol
Painted by E. HARRISON COMPTON. Des-
cribed by W. A. BAILLIE-GROHMAN. 24
Full-Page Illustrations in Colour.

PUBLISHED BY A. AND C. BLACK · SOHO SQUARE · LONDON · W.

AND OBTAINABLE THROUGH ANY BOOKSELLER AT HOME OR ABROAD

BLACK'S BEAUTIFUL BOOKS
ALL WITH FULL-PAGE ILLUSTRATIONS IN COLOUR

FOR ANGLERS

By Post, Price 7s. 11d.   **PRICE 7s. 6d. NET EACH**   Size 8 × 5½ ins.

Fishermen's Weather
Edited by F. G. AFLALO. Opinions and Experiences by 100 well-known Anglers. Containing 8 Full-Page Illustrations in Colour from Pictures by CHARLES WHYMPER, F.Z.S.

Trout Fishing
By W. EARL HODGSON. Third Edition. Containing Frontispiece and a Model Book of Flies in Colour.

Salmon Fishing
By W. EARL HODGSON. Containing 8 Full-Page Illustrations in Colour, including Model Cases of 74 Varieties of Salmon Flies, and 10 Full-Page Reproductions from Photographs.

MISCELLANEOUS

China
Painted by MORTIMER MENPES. Text by THE HON. SIR HENRY ARTHUR BLAKE, G.C.M.G. 16 Full-Page Illustrations in Colour and many Line Drawings in the Text. Demy Quarto, Cloth, Gilt Top.

PRICE 5s. NET; by Post, Price 5s. 6d.

The Ramparts of Empire
Painted by NORMAN L. WILKINSON. Text by FRANK FOX. 12 Full-Page Illustrations in Colour. Large Crown Octavo, Cloth.

PRICE 5s. NET; by Post, Price 5s. 4d.

Oriental Carpets, Runners and Rugs, and some Jacquard Reproductions
By SYDNEY HUMPHRIES. 24 Full-Page Reproductions in Colour and 8 Full-Page Illustrations in Black and White. Demy Quarto, Cloth, Gilt Top.

PRICE £2 2s. NET; by Post, Price £2 2s. 9d.

Gainsborough
Engraved by MORTIMER MENPES. Text by JAMES GREIG, R.B.A. 15 Full-Page Examples of the Master's Work in Colour-Facsimile. Imperial Quarto, Cloth, Gilt Top. (Size 15 × 11 inches.)

PRICE £3 3s. NET; by Post, Price £3 3s. 9d.

THE "MOTOR ROUTES" SERIES
By GORDON HOME

The Motor Routes of England
A Guide to the Beautiful Scenery and Interesting Localities in the Country

SOUTHERN SECTION (South of the Thames)
Large Crown Octavo. Containing 24 Full-Page Illustrations in Colour, and 45 Sketch Maps in the Text.

WESTERN SECTION
Large Crown Octavo. Containing 24 Full-Page Illustrations in Colour and 42 Sketch Maps in the Text.
In preparation.

Cloth, Each Price 5s. Net (by Post, Price 5s. 5d.); Leather, Each Price 7s. 6d. Net (by Post, Price 7s. 11d.)

The Motor Routes of France. Part I.
To the Châteaux Country, Biarritz, The Pyrenees, The Riviera, and the Rhone Valley

Large Crown Octavo. Containing 16 Full-Page Illustrations in Colour, 16 in Black and White, and 63 Maps and Plans.

Cloth, Price 5s. Net (by Post, Price 5s. 5d.); Leather, Price 7s. 6d. Net (by Post, Price 7s. 11d.)

Rembrandt
By MORTIMER MENPES. With an Essay on the Life and Work of Rembrandt by C. LEWIS HIND. Demy Quarto, Cloth, Gilt Top (11 × 8¼ inches). 16 Examples of the Master's Work, Reproduced in Colour-Facsimile by a Special Process.

PRICE 12s. 6d. NET ; by Post, Price 13s.

The Lady of the Lake
By SIR WALTER SCOTT. Large Crown Octavo, Cloth, Gilt Top. 50 Full-Page Illustrations (8 of them in Colour, from Paintings by SUTTON PALMER).

PRICE 5s. NET
By Post, Price 5s. 5d.

The Practical Angler
Or, The Art of Trout Fishing, more particularly applied to Clear Water
By W. C. STEWART. Large Crown Octavo, Cloth. Containing Coloured Facsimiles of the Flies used by Mr. STEWART (6 Plates).

PRICE 3s. 6d. NET
By Post, Price 3s. 10d.

THE "PORTRAIT BIOGRAPHIES" SERIES.
Sir Henry Irving
By MORTIMER and DOROTHY MENPES. Containing 8 Portraits of Irving in Colour. (Size 6¼ × 4 ins.)

PRICE 2s. NET
By Post, Price 2s. 3d.

THE "PEOPLES OF MANY LANDS" SERIES

Each Large Fcap. Quarto (9 × 7½ ins.). Cloth, Price 5s. net each; by Post, Price 5s. 4d.

The People of Holland
Painted by NICO JUNGMAN. Containing 32 Full-Page Plates in Colour, Tipped on Grey Mounts, and the Interleaves with Descriptive Notes Quaintly Ornamented.

The People of Egypt
Painted by LANCE THACKERAY. Containing 32 Full-Page Plates in Colour, Tipped on Grey Mounts, and the Interleaves, with the Descriptive Notes Illustrated with Thumb-nail Sketches in Black and White.

The People of India
Painted by MORTIMER MENPES. Containing 32 Full-Page Plates in Colour, Tipped on Grey Mounts.

A DETAILED PROSPECTUS, containing a specimen plate, of any volume in this List will be sent on application to the Publishers.

PUBLISHED BY A. AND C. BLACK · SOHO SQUARE · LONDON · W.
AND OBTAINABLE THROUGH ANY BOOKSELLER AT HOME OR ABROAD